German Helicopters WW2

By Leo Lindberg

Foreword

The treaty of Versailles which ended the Great War, known to us today as the World War I was designed to keep Germany a poor nation. To keep German and Austrian agression contained, by taking every one of Germanys colonies, protectorates and remove as many parts of the German and the Austrian-Hungarian state.

As we know this did not succeed. Instead this created dissent and animosity towards the victors of World War I.

Another thing resulting from the Versailles treaty was German ingenuity. Specially in the aviation industry. Many of the German aircraft designers formed company's in different countries like Sweden and the Soviet Union were they tried there revolutionary designs. Later when the Nazi's took power the designers returned to Germany and in the 30's Germany was the leading place for research and development of aircraft designs and helicopters.

Part of this revolution was of because funding of the different projects and a government focused on rearmament of its army, navy and air force.

In these projects which were many, not only in the aircraft industry, was several projects of aircraft which could make vertical lift off.

Projects by Henrich Focke, Anton Flettner and Von Doblhof . These ingenious designs would influence British, French and American helicopter designs after the world war II.

The ingenious designs made in very few numbers lacked only one thing. The Germans never really considered how to use the helicopters, they never really came up with a doctrine for usage. By chance they noted helicopters were useful for transporting cargo in the mountains, but rather late they noted that it would be useful in other terrain too.

This is an overview of the different German helicopter projects of World War II.

Focke-Achgelis Fa 223
Focke-Achgelis Fa 225
Flettner Fl 185
Flettner Fl 265
Flettner Fl 282
Flettner Fl 330
Doblhof WNF 342

Focke-Wulf Fw 61

Fw 61 test without fabric covered tubular fuselage

The credit for much of the German rotorcraft industry's development lay with Henrich Focke. Together with Georg Wulf, Focke founded the Focke-Wulf aircraft company in 1923. In its early years, Focke-Wulf developed several commercially unsuccessful fixed-wing aircraft (Wulf was killed while flight testing during this period), before producing the popular Fw 44 Stieglitz in 1934. During this time, Focke had also purchased a license to build autogyros from the Cierva Autogyro Company, and created over 30 of the aircraft. This experience helped him in the development of his own helicopter which was the Fw 61.

The Fw 61, powered by a 160hp Siemens-Halske Sh 14 radial engine, it was a single-seat design, with counter-rotating twin rotors set on outriggers on either side of the fuselage. The first fully controllable helicopter, it was capable of flying forwards, sideways, and backwards — and was able to hover. It took its first tethered flight in June 1936, and in May 1937, carried out one of the world's first autorotational landings, from a height of 1,130 feet (344 meters). Two months later, the Fw 61 broke helicopter records when it flew at 76 mph (122 km/h) to reach an altitude of 11,243 feet (3,426 meters), and flew non-stop for 143 miles (230 kilometers).

The Fw 61 had an airframe from the Focke-Wulf Fw 44 Stieglitz (Goldfinch) training plane.At each side of its fuselage it had boom in a triagular form mounted, carrying one of the two rotor heads on its tip. Each of the rotors had a diameter of 7.5m, so that the helicopter had a span of more than 15m.

Fw 61, flown by Hanna Reitsch. Focke-Wulf Fw 61

The Fw 61 is often considered the first practical, functional helicopter. It was also known as the Fa 61, as Focke began a new company Focke Achgelis for helicopter manufacture after development had begun

The Fw 61 garnered great publicity when Hannah Reitsch, a young female test pilot, flew the aircraft inside the Deutschlandhalle sports arena in Berlin in 1938, and U.S. aviation pioneer Charles Lindbergh was even given a demonstration of its capabilities during a pre-war visit to the country. Helicopter development soared in Germany at this time — and across the Atlantic, funding was released for U.S. helicopter development. Unfortunately, neither of the two Fw 61s produced would survive the war.

Photo of the Fw flying in the Deutschland Halle in Berlin

Two prototypes were built Fw 61V1 (D-EBVU) and FW 61V2 (D-EKRA). Both were flown with success by Edgar Rohlfs, Karl Bode and Hanna Reitsch. Later Diplo. Ing. Karl Franke of Rechlin test center joined the test team. Hanna Reitsch and Karl Franke kept discovering new capabilities of the Fw 61. This led to Hanna Reitsch flying the Fw61 at a public event inside the Deutschland Halle.in Berlin. This was part of a car show. The spectators at the time did not know what they had witnessed. Experts inside and outside Germany knew what kind of progress Germany had accomplished with the Fw 61. Germany broke all records for helicopters with this Focke-Wulf design.

Hanna Reitsch piloting the Fw 61 V2 D-EKRA, 1938

The prototype Focke-Achelis Fw 61 first took flight on June 26, 1936

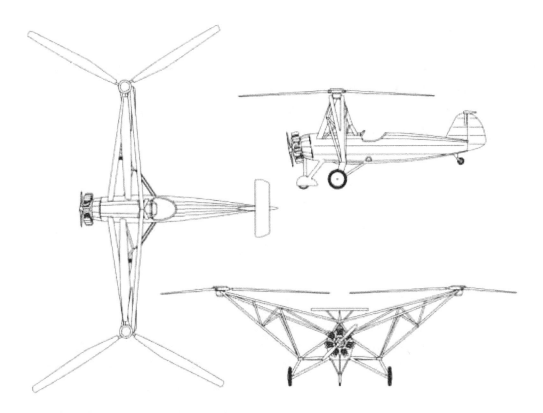

Controls

The Fw 61 had two side by side (transverse mounted) counter-rotating three-bladed rotors, each mounted on a set of struts. Two connected the rotor to the undercarriage. Three connected the rotor to a point on the side of the fuselage just behind the engine, with the middle of these struts carrying a shaft that connected the engine to the rotor. Finally another strut led to a connection mounted just above the centre of the fuselage. The counter-rotating rotors cancelled out each others torque, and so the Fw 61 didn't need a tail rotor.

On modern helicopters height is controlled using collective pitch, where the angle of all propeller blades are adjusted by the same amount at the same time, increasing or decreasing the amount of lift they generate and causing the helicopter to rise or fall. On the Fw 61 height was controlled by using the throttle to alter rotor speed.

Horizontal movement was producing using cyclic pitch, where the angle of each blade changed as it rotated. If no other controls are in use then each blade on both rotors would be at the same angle at the same positions. Adjusting cyclic pitch means that the rotor produces a different amount of lift in different places on the disc, causing it to tilt, and thus generate movement.

Differential cyclic pitch was used to spin the helicopter. Here the two rotors would be adjusted in opposite ways - if the lift was increased at the front of the right-hand rotor then it would be decreased at the front of the left hand rotor. The two rotors would tilt in opposite directions and the Fw 61 would spin.

Differential collective pitch was used to tilt the helicopter to left or right. Here the angle of every blade on one rotor would be altered by one amount and every blade on the other rotor by a different amount. The two rotors would thus produce different amounts of lift, and the Fw 61 would spin.

Fw 61V1 and V2 where the first helicopters that could take-off and land vertically

The Success of the Fw61 resulted in the granting of a Luftwaffe contract for development of a helicopter that should be capable of carrying a payload of 700kg. This was done in Bremen and Delmenhorst.

Timeline

The Fw 61 V1 made its maiden flight on 26 June 1936 with test pilot Ewald Rohlf at the controls. Focke recorded the test flight as lasting for 45 seconds, while other records said 28 seconds.

The Fw 61 was flown by a number of test pilots, include the famous Hann Reitsch, Rohlfs, Karl Bode and Karl Franke.

The Fw 61 established a whole series of rotor craft records, although by the time this began the aircraft had been redesignated as the Focke-Achgelis Fa 61.

On 25 June 1937 Ewald Rohlfs set a height record of 8,000ft and stayed in the air for 1hr 20min.

On 26 June 1937 Rohlfs set a straight line distance record of 10.19 miles, a closed-circuit speed record of 76.15mph and a closed-circuir distance record of 50.09 miles.

On 25 October 1937 Hann Reitsch raised the straight-line distance record to 67.67 miles (From Breman to Berlin).

In February 1938 Hanna Reitsch flew the Fa 61 inside the Deutschlandhalle in front of a large crowd. Most people in the crowd were impressed by the flight, but were unaware of its true significance, which was that the Fa 61 was considered to be reliable enough and controllable enough to fly over a large crowd in a confined success. The flight signalled the success of the Fa 61 to the wider aeronautical world.

In 20 June 1938 Karl Bode raised the straight line record yet again, this time to 143.05 miles.

On 29 January 1939 Bode raised the altitude record to 11,240.5ft. This was the last official record set before the outbreak of the Second World War.

The success of the Fa 61 led to an order for a new passenger carrying version of the helicopter, and the eventual development of the Focke-Achgelis Fa 266 and military Focke-Achgelis Fa 223. Focke also had plans for a two-seat sports version, the Focke-Achgelis Fa 224, but this was abandoned after the outbreak of the Second World War.

Focke-Achgelis Fa 223 DRACHE

Henrich Focke with a model of the Fa 223 Drache

Late in 1938, the German Navy requested a much larger and more powerful helicopter which could be used for protecting convoys and as a substitute for E-boats in mine-laying and torpedo attacks, and design of the Fa 223 Drache was initiated. A helicopter with extremely advanced capabilities for its time, the Fa 223 was fundamentally an extension of the concept which had produced the smaller Fw 61 and employed a generally similar arrangement of twin counter-rotating rotors mounted on outriggers from the main airframe and driven by a fuselage-mounted radial engine. In the case of the Fa 223, however, the engine was installed in the middle of the fuselage in the fabric-covered steel-tube to the rear of the 4-seat passenger compartment. The forward part of this cabin was a multiple-panelled enclosure made up of flat Plexiglas panels, and the aircraft was fitted with a tricycle undercarriage. Usual powerplant was a 1000hp Bramo 323Q3 radial engine.

With this project professor Focke withdrew from the Focke-Wulf company to dedicated himself to this project with the renowned pilot Gerd Achgelis. In August 1939 the Fa

233V1(V was for Versuch (Experiment)) left the assembly line. The first test runs showed problems, and it took almost a year solve the problems to make the first flight. Series production began in 1942.

The first prototype, the Fa 223V1 which bore the civil registration D-OCEB, was completed in the summer of 1939; and after a 100.hour ground test, the first test flight was made on August 3, 1940. The Fa 223V1, like its predecessor, had side- by-side three-bladed rotors mounted laterally on steel-tube outrigger arms. The welded steel-tube fuselage was fabric-covered and accommodated a crew of two in an extensively glazed nose. Behind the flight compartment was a cabin for four passengers or freight, and aft of this was situated the engine bay which contained a 980hp BMW 323 air-cooled radial mounted on flexible rubber supports, and driving the rotors by means of shafts through a friction clutch from the engine crankshaft. During an examination at the Rechlin test centre on October 28, 1940, the Fa 223V1, with Karl Bode at the controls, and ballast to the equivalent of a full payload, attained an altitude of 23,294 feet. At this altitude, the helicopter's climb rate was still between l00 and 200 ft./min. The spectacular results of these altitude tests- which were closely guarded secrets at the time resulted in the suggestion that the Fa 223 should be used for an attempt to climb Mount Everest. The maximum level speed attained during the Rechlin tests was 115.5 mph.

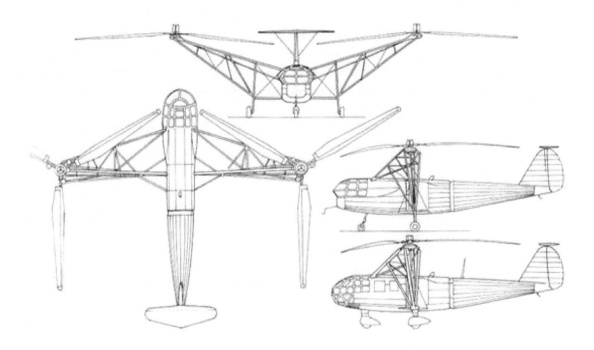

Some difficulties were experienced with torsional vibration resulting from the rotors revolving out of phase. The second prototype, the Fa 223V2 (D-OGAW), incorporated all the experience gained during the testing of the first machine, and offered substantial improvements. At one time, two-blade rotors were tested. This machine was intended for a new helicopter speed record, and it was anticipated that a level speed of 137 mph would be reached, however, before the full speed range of the helicopter had been examined, the machine was destroyed in a bombing attack.

Thee machine was subjected to the most stringent tests lifting and moving a 7.5cm PaK(antitank gun), supplying a mountain battery with ammunition and supplies, a job that normally required 40 to 50 mules. A whole battery of 7.5 mountain infantry guns were moved from a valley to a 2000 meter high mountain position by a single Fa 223.
In1944 two Fa 223's were stationed in Münster as recovery and rescue aircraft, which would move crews and aircraft. In one case, the motor of a Focke-Wulf FW 190 weighing 1284 kg was moved a distance of 32 km.

In the meantime, production of an initial series of one hundred helicopters bad been initiated for the German armed forces, under the designation Fa 223E Drache, at Delrnenhorst and Oxenhausen. The Fa 223E was generally similar to the Fa 223V2 but featured several modifications to suit it for military duties. Bulky loads could be attached beneath the fuselage, enabling cargoes to be picked up and set down without landing. Among test loads were a military Volkswagen Kubelwagen and a disassembled Fieseler Fi 156C Storch monoplane. Normally, a 1,000 h.p. Bramo 323Q-3 engine was installed, and in 1944, a two-stage supercharger was fitted, and tests undertaken with water-methanol injection which boosted maximum output to 1,200 hp. During one test, a Fa 223E carried a 1,100-lb. load to the top of the "Dresdener Hütte " (7,546 ft.), near Mittenwald, Karwendel. Torpedo dropping tests were not successful, however.
Production of the Drache began at the end of 1941 (with entry into service at the beginning of 1942) and ceased in 1945 with a total of 43 aircraft, in addition to the 11 prototypes. As the Allies destroyed most of the production sites, only 20 examples of the world's first truly operational helicopter.

Focke-Achgelis Fa 223 DRACHE

Unfortunately, the majority of the Fa 223E helicopters were destroyed by bombing during the final assault on Germany but one was flown across the Channel (being the first helicopter to perform this feat) and tested in England, although it crashed after a few days in the test programme and was a total write-off.

SNCASE SE3000 was built on the basis of the German Focke Achgelis Fa-223 Drache helicopter with the direct participation of Professor Focke. The first flight of the helicopter, equipped with 1000 hp BMW-323 Bramo Fafnir engines, took place on October 23, 1948 SE-3000. Another was reconstructed by the Avia factory in Czechoslovakia for tests under the designation VR-1.

The earliest military helicopters were built by Germany and mainly saw service in the Mediterranean, but a few were also used in the Aegean and Baltic theatres. Both the Flettner 282 and the Focke Achgelis Fa 223 (shown here) were never built in large numbers as a result of the production facilities being destroyed by Allied bombers

A Focke Achgelis FA 223, considered to be the largest and most efficient helicopter of the 1940s, was based on the principle of the FW 61. They distinguished themselves especially by their quality as a transport and resupply helicopter

Focke-Achgelis Fa 223, was armed with a 7.92 mm MG15. It had a crew of two and was substantially larger than the other early types, it came into service in 1942, around the same time as the Fl 282

Fa 223 making tests in the mountains, moving artillery

September 6, 1945: A captured German Focke-Achgelis Fa 223 V14, makes the first helicopter crossing of the English Channel when it is moved from Cherbourg to RAF Beaulieu. The US had intended to ferry two captured aircraft back to the USA aboard a ship, but only had room for one

Luftwaffe helicopter pilot Helmut Gerstenhauer, with two observers, flew another aircraft across the Channel to the base in Hampshire

Focke-Achgelis Fa 223 V12 Drache, 1940 cargo helicopter

A captured helicopter. Focke-Achgelis Fa 223 Drache. A single 750 kilowatt (1,000 horsepower) Bramo 323 radial engine powered two three-bladed 11.9-meter (39 feet) rotors mounted on twin booms on either side of the 12.2-meter (40 ft) long cylindrical fuselage.

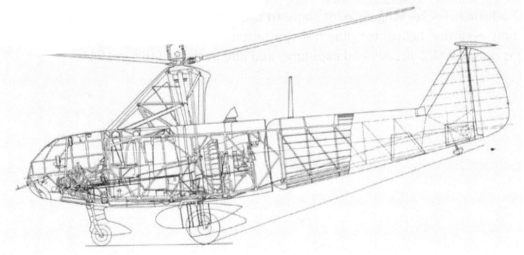

Cutaway of the Fa 233

In 1952 a former Focke-Achgelis pilot came to the USA. He amazed the Americans, who at the time regarded helicopter sling transportation as impossible with the fact that the Germans during WW2 already had experimented and perfected this in 1944.

The US intended to ferry captured aircraft back to the US aboard a ship, but only had room for one of the captured Drache. The RAF objected to plans to destroy the other, the V14, so Gerstenhauer, with two observers, flew it across the English Channel from Cherbourg to RAF Beaulieu on 6 September 1945, the first crossing of the Channel by a helicopter. The V14 later made two test flights at RAF Beaulieu before being destroyed on 3 October in a crash where the helicopter dropped 18 meters to the ground. The isue that led to the crash was that every 25 hours, the steel housing securing the engine should be tightened using a special tool, but that tool was never brought to England. Despite Gerstenhauer's warnings, the tests had continued, this lead to the driveshaft failure and the crashof the Fa223V14.

A Fa 223 Dragon in English colours

A French produced SNCASE SE3000

In France, the Sud-Est company constructed the SE.3000 as a development of the Fa 223, assisted by Focke. Designed for transport purposes, it had accommodation for four passengers and was powered by one 1000hp BMW-323-R2 engine. Three were built. The Prototype F-WFDR flew the first time on the 23 Oct. 1948.

This SE.3000 is a development of the German helicopter Fa 223. Incidentally, Professor Focke himself took part in building the aircraft. Principally designed for transport purposes, this helicopter carried, in addition to the two-man crew, four passengers in a cabin situated behind the pilot's seat. This cabin was forward of the engine compartment. The aircraft was also equipped with a weight-lifting mechanism, which really turned it into a helicrane.

The fuselage was constructed of welded steel tubing. It was fitted with a fin and a rudder. The rotors, the centres of which were 12.5 metres apart, were carried on cantilever outriggers.

Like France the Czechoslovak government was highly interested in the Fa 223, and they produced three from parts and used them for testing. After testing was finished they used by the Czechoslovak police and border guards. In Czechoslovak service the Fa 223 was known as the VR-1.

The Czechoslovak produced Avia VR-1

Fa 223A: for anti-submarine warfare, to carry 2 × 250 kg (550 lb) bombs or depth charges

Fa 223B: for reconnaissance missions; fitted with an auxiliary drop tank

Fa 223C: for search and rescue duties, fitted with a steel winch cable

Fa 223D: freight variant, for resupplying mountain troops

Fa 223E: dual-control trainer

Fa 223Z: A hybrid Fa 223 was proposed by Focke with two fuselages joined inline to form a four-rotor heavy lift helicopter. An unfinished central joining section was found by Allied troops at Ochsenhausen.

SE.3000: postwar French production

VR-1: postwar Czechoslovak production

Crew: 2

Capacity: 4 passengers

Length: 12.25 m (40 ft 2 in) fuselage length

Wingspan: 24.50 m (80 ft 5 in) span over rotors

Height: 4.36 m (14 ft 4 in)

Empty weight: 3,180 kg (7,011 lb)

Gross weight: 3,860 kg (8,510 lb)

Max takeoff weight: 4,315 kg (9,513 lb)

Fuel capacity: 490 L (108 Imp gal) internal + 300 L (66 Imp gal) external tank

Powerplant: 1 × BMW Bramo 323D-2 nine-cylinder radial, 750 kW (1,000 hp) at take-off

Maximum speed: 176 km/h (109 mph, 95 kn) at 2,000 m (6,600 ft)

Cruise speed: 134 km/h (83 mph, 72 kn) at 2,000 m (6,600 ft)

Range: 437 km (272 mi, 236 nmi) internal fuel

Ferry range: 700 km (430 mi, 380 nmi) with auxiliary fuel

Endurance: 2 hr 20 min

Service ceiling: 4,875 m (15,994 ft) service ceiling

Rate of climb: 4.1 m/s (800 ft/min) (vertical rate of climb), 5.6 m/s (1,100 ft/min) with forward speed

Armament

Guns: 1×MG 15 machine gun manually aimed from the nose.

Bombs: 2×250 kg (550 lb) bombs or 2×depth charges

Focke-Achgelis Fa 225

The Focke-Achgelis Fa 225 was an experimental single-seat rotary wing glider built in Nazi Germany by Focke-Achgelis in 1942. Only a single example was constructed.

Rare photo of Focke-Achgelis Fa 225, German experimental rotary wing glider of 1942 constructed from the fuselage of a DFS.230 glider, with the wings replaced by a Fa 223 rotor. This is the only one ever built. Note the camouflage paint

In the first half of the Second World War, the DFS 230B assault glider was used primarily to land troops and supplies, but was found of limited capability as it had only a small carrying capacity. The Fa 225 was conceived to marry the rotor of the Focke-Achgelis Fa 223 with the fuselage of the DFS 230B, allowing the glider to land in 18m or less. The rotor was mounted on a framework of struts above the centre of gravity and strengthened long stroke undercarriage units were fitted either side and at the tail.

Towed behind a Junkers Ju 52/3m, Karl Bode piloted the Fa 225 on its first flight in 1943. Construction of the aircraft only took seven weeks, but series production was not proceeded with due to the relatively slow aero-towing speed and changes in operational doctrine.

The Fa 225 was the fuselage of a DFS 230 transport glider married to a Fa 223 rotor head. This was intended to serve as an assault glider for use in confined spaces, but tests were not entirely successful and development was abandoned.

The Fa 225 was without an engine, with the rotor mounted on the fuselage of the DFS230 glider, which used the rotor to create lift instead of its wings. Other test with the Fa 225 a Heinkel He 45 was used to tow the rotor glider into the air. Test were made to land and make take-off at very steep angles with no trouble.

The Fa 225 was to be used as one of the 9 gliders in the mountain raid on Gran Rosso to rescue Benito Mussolini, because there was so little space to land an ordinary DFS230 glider. During test landing the Fa 225, was damaged and could not be used to fly the assault team. This resulted in the legendary escape of Mussolini and Skorzeny in a Fieseler Fi 156 Storch(Stork), where Skorzeny threatened the Luftwaffe pilot to take Mussolini and himself of Gran Rosso, although the Storch only could manage to lift the pilot and Mussolini in theory.

From the development of the Fa 225, came the idea for the Fa 330.

Crew: 1
Capacity: 9 paratroopers
Length: 11.24 m (36 ft 11 in) fuselage only
Max takeoff weight: 2,000 kg)
Main rotor diameter: 12 m
Maximum speed: 190 km/h (120 mph, 100 kn) during towing by Ju 52/3m

Focke-Achgelis Fa 330

The Focke-Achgelis FA 330 Bachstelze (English: Water Wagtail) was a type of rotary-wing kite, known as a gyro glider or rotor kite. They were towed behind German U-boats during World War II to allow a lookout to see farther as a sort of scout.

It was a small light gyroplane, designed for use on ships. The airstream of the ship was supposed to suffice to allow the Fa 330 to lift up. By the end of World War II, some 200 of these small, motorless, three-bladed autogyros had been built for Focke Achgelis by the Weser Flugzeugwerke at Delmenhorst. This rotorcraft was flown as a kite towed by a submarine from a cable 60 to 150 metres in length. The collapsible assembly was made of steel tubes, and just behind the pilot's seat was a pylon to support the rotor. The latter's hub was of the simplest possible autogyro type with flapping and drag hinges. The rotor was set in motion by a rope or by hand alone, if there was sufficient wind blowing. To bring the autogyro back, the towing rope was pulled in by winch, and when the aircraft landed the rotor was brought to a standstill with a brake.

A Wagtail in use. Development was completed by August 1942. In April 1943, one was deployed to the Indian Ocean aboard U-177, a long-range Type IXD2 U-boat

Training to handle this autogyro was given in a wind tunnel at Ghalais Meudon in France. An original Fa 330 is still preserved in the French Air Museum.

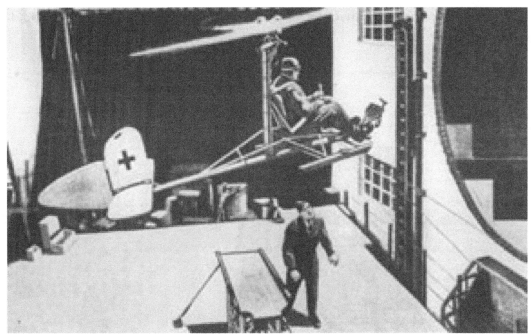

Pilot training by flying the Fa 330 in a full scale wind tunnel at Chalais-Meudon, France

Early in 1942, Focke Achgelis at Laupheim were asked to design a simple single-seat gyro kite which surfaced U-boats could tow aloft to extend the observer's range of view. At this time, the U-boats were being forced away from the dense shipping areas around the coasts of Britain and the United States to hunt further out into the Atlantic where there was greater safety, but where their low position in the water made searching for, and shadowing, the spread-out convoys a very difficult task unless a bosun's chair could be attached to the periscope.

Fa 330 on Uboat

The gyro kite, designated Fa 330 Bachstelze, was seen as some sort of solution and ingenuity was shown in its design. The machine could be easily assembled or dismantled in a few minutes and stowed through a U-boat hatch. The body structure consisted of two main steel tubes, one horizontal and one vertical. On the horizontal tube was mounted the pilot's seat with controls and a small instrument panel, and landing skids, and, at the rear end, a simple tailplane, fin and rudder. The vertical tube, behind the pilot's seat, formed a pylon for the rotor.

Uboat crew readying a Fa 330 for take-off

The freely-rotating rotor had three blades, each of which consisted of a tubular-steel spar with plywood ribs and thin plywood and fabric covering. Each rotor blade had flapping and dragging hinges with adjustable dampers. Blade pitch could only be adjusted, with screws, on the ground before take-off. The best results were normally obtained with the blade pitch as coarse as possible, although starting was then more difficult. In addition to the flapping and dragging dampers, there were also inter blade connecting cables and blade-droop cables, the latter being attached to the blades and to an inverted tripod extending upward from the rotor hub. The rotor axis was slightly ahead of the machine's center of Gravity, and the towing cable attachment point was slightly ahead and below the center of Gravity.

Movement of the control column tilted the rotor head in the appropriate direction for longitudinal and lateral control, and operation of the rudder pedals gave directional control. The tailplane was not adjustable. The Fa 330 was launched from the deck of the surface-running U-boat by giving the machine a slight backwards tilt once the rotor was revolving. If there was a wind, a push by hand sufficed to get the rotor moving, but otherwise a pull-rope was wound around a grooved drum on the rotor hub. In case this rope did not slip off when the rotor started, an over-ride mechanism was fitted.

Pilot training was given in a wind-tunnel at Chalais-Meudon near Paris, and the kite was very easy to operate and could be flown hands-off for up to 10 seconds. It is believed that two or three crew members of each Fa 330 equipped U-boat learned to fly it.

Having 150m of towing cable available, it was possible to maintain an altitude of 120m thereby extending the possible range of vision very usefully to 40km compared with only 8km on the U-boat deck. In an emergency, the pilot, who had telephone contact with the U-boat, pulled a lever over his head which jettisoned the rotor and released the towing cable. As the rotor flew away and up, it pulled out a parachute mounted behind the pylon. At this stage, the pilot, attached to the parachute, unfastened his safety belt to allow the remainder of the Fa 330 to fall into the sea while he made a normal parachute descent. In a normal descent, the kite was winched in to the deck and, upon landing, the rotor brake applied.

Although designed by Focke Achgelis, the Fa 330 was built by the Weser-Flugzeugbau at Hoykenkamp, near Bremen. This particular factory manufactured Focke-Wulf Fw 190 fuselages, a few Fa 223 helicopters and about two hundred Fa 330s. Variations made in the basic design were an increase in rotor diameter to 8.53m on late machines and the option of adding simple landing wheels to the skids. There was also a proposal, designated Fa 336, to build a powered version of the Fa 330 with landing wheels and a 60hp engine.

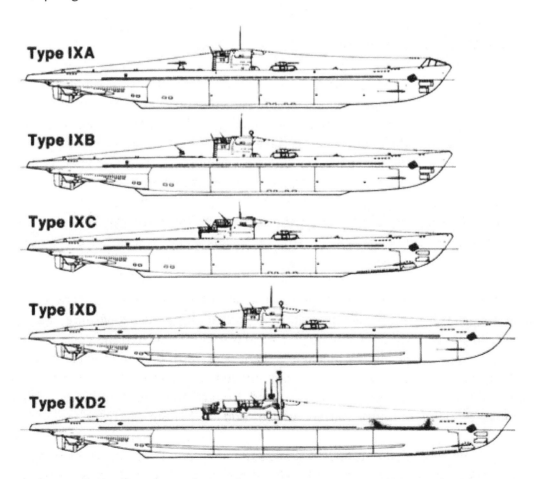

Type IXA

Type IXB

Type IXC

Type IXD

Type IXD2

The principal U-boat class to use the Fa 330 was the ocean-going Type IX which had a surface displacement of 1050-1610 tons, a surface speed of 18 to 21 kt and a submerged speed of 6.9 to 7.7kt. Among the operational U-boats of the Kriegsmarine, only the Type IX-D/2 supply U-boat had a faster surface speed of 21 kt, and this type was used with the Fa 330. Little is known of actual operations with the kite, or how many were issued, but there is no doubt that the use of the gyro kite was unpopular, because, in an emergency, the U-boat had either to delay its dive in order to pick up the kite's pilot, or dive and hope to pick him up later. The advantages of a self-propelled machine seem clear. The first Fa 330s were probably issued in mid 1942 but were used in the South Atlantic only on rare occasions. From June 1942, the harried U-boat forces swung their main effort from the Atlantic to the Gulf of Aden and the Indian Ocean, where more use of the gyro kite was made. U-861, for example, used her kite on a patrol in the Indian Ocean off Madagascar. However, the new theatre of operations provided opportunities to exchange the Fa 330 for, in the eyes of the commander, something more usable. At Penang, Malaya, the Japanese had permitted the establishment of a U-boat base in the summer of 1943, and it was here that an Fa 330 was exchanged for a small Japanese floatplane. On another occasion, at ihe Surabaya (Java) U boat base, a gyro kite was exchanged for a Japanese floatplane to supplement the two Arado reconnaissance aircraft which kept watch over the harbour.

Focke-Achgelis Fa 330

Crew: 1
Length 4.47 m
Height (spur on the ground)   1.67 m (2.40 m)
Rotor diameter   7.3 m
Rotor area   42.0 m²
Storage space in the submarine   2.0 m³ (3.57 m long)
Setup weight of the aircraft   75 kg

Guide with special clothing   90 kg
and life jacket .
Parachute   10 kg
All-up weight 175 kg
Rotor area loading   4.2 kg / m²
Speed range   35 to 80 km / h
(Ride + wind) .
greatest altitude   220 m (300 m rope)
Viewing area   about 35 to 53 km
Descent time   about 4 min
Dismantling and stowing time   about 7 min
Dismantling time   about 7 min
Rate of descent at 40 km / h about 3.5 m / s
Best glide angle in free flight 1: 4.5

The compact single man aircraft, with its 24-foot (7.3-meter) three-bladed rotor, could be assembled in minutes, and flew up to a height of 500 feet (152 meters). The pilot communicated with the U-boat below by telephone line running down the tow cable. The Fa 330 was normally winched back down to the submarine; however, in an emergency, the autogyro cable could be cut and the pilot could parachute to safety as the aircraft fell into the ocean.

The Fa 330 autogyros were placed in service during 1942. Some were used in the Indian Ocean, while a few also went to Japan

With the gyroplane Focke-Achgelis Fa 330 Wagtail, the Focke-Achgelis company in Delmenhorst achieved an interesting development during the Second World War, the basic principle of which is still practiced today for remote observation from the air.

The visibility of a watercraft, especially a low-built submarine, is known to be very limited. On the other hand, at that time, when long-range location and radar devices were still in development, it was particularly difficult for submarines to detect more distant targets and enemy submarines in good time. Since the installation of high masts was practically impossible and the accompaniment of reconnaissance aircraft was associated with many disadvantages and almost insoluble problems, a device was developed that could be raised from the boat and retracted as required.

The German Focke-Achgelis Fa 330 "Bachstelze" was a small motorless gyroplane intended for use on submarines and ships. The machines could start at a speed of 30 km/h. They were propelled and lifted up (autorotation) solely by the speed of the submarine and by the wind .

The structure was extremely simple and consisted of a tubular steel construction and a main rotor measuring 7.31 m in diameter, which consisted of three rotor blades. The gyroplanes could be folded up. They were not stowed in the interiors of the ships or submarines, but in two large (60 cm diameter) pressure vessels that were lockable with watertight lids and that were mounted vertically on the tower of the submarine. One of the containers contained the three rotor blades and the hub, the other fuselage structure, controls and tail unit.

The start took place from a start table which was mounted in the winter garden of the submarine. The individual observer had a greatly increased range of vision, which should improve the location of targets. It took seven minutes to get the machines ready for use on a submarine, and they were packed in two minutes. In emergencies, the pilot could drop the rotor and then land with the rest of the machine hanging from a parachute. More than 112 of these simple but highly technical devices for its time were built and used on the type IX D 2 submarines.

An attempt to expand the view without the Fa 330 Bachstelze

Construction description (excerpts from the original manual)

1. Fuselage:

The fuselage frame is welded together from thin-walled steel tubes. It consists of a longitudinal tube that is reinforced in the front area by a lattice girder on which the seat cushion is attached.

The equipment board is detachable connected to the front end of the longitudinal tube. The rudder log, the tow rope coupling with release handle,the front starting slide mounting and the control stick mounting are also located on the front part of the longitudinal tube. The fittings for the seat upholstery, the waist belt and the supports for the starter sledge and head carrier are welded to the lattice girder, as well as a handle for the left hand. Next to the handle is the handle for the brake of the rotary wing.

Behind the seat, the longitudinal tube carries the fittings for the rear launching sled bearing and the head carrier, and at the rear end the connection fittings for the horizontal and vertical fin, as well as for the spur.

2. landing gear

In the case of land or sea use, the aircraft has a slide for take-off and landing on the take-off table. In special cases (free flight with landing on land) the starter sledge can be exchanged for a landing gear. Removal and installation is quick and easy.

a) Start sled
The launch slide for sea use is used to store the machine during take-off and landing. After releasing a lock, it can be swiveled to the side member for stowage. The starting slide consists of a front and a rear rotary lever, the two skids and the right and left V-braces.
b) Land landing gear
The land landing gear consists of the chassis and the spur. There is no landing gear brake system.

3. Tail

The tail unit consists of the horizontal stabilizer, the vertical fin and the rudder. It is made of tubular steel and covered with fabric. Rapid assembly and dismantling is made possible by quick-release fasteners.

Horizontal stabilizer
The horizontal stabilizer is arranged just above the longitudinal tube. The spar, which also forms the leading edge of the fin, is supported at two points by catches on the fuselage. The third bracket, which is inserted into a cutout in the fin bracket, is in the middle of the trailing edge.

Fin
The covering of the fin leaves the lower ends of the front and end spars free, which are inserted into two tubular supports at the end of the fuselage. A catch keeps the front spar - and with it the whole fin - in place. The trailing edge carries the bearing for the rudder at the top.

Rudder
The rudder spar, which at the same time forms the leading edge of the rudder, has a catch at its upper end for mounting and suspending the rudder on the fin. At its lower end there is a transverse lever with two welded pins to transfer the control forces, which grip from below into the corresponding bores of the rudder lever and thus simultaneously form the second bearing of the rudder.

4. Control unit

The control unit consists of the hand control and the foot control, which are operated in the same way as on a normal aircraft . With the manual control, the rotary wing axis is tilted backwards (pulling) or forwards (pushing) in the longitudinal direction of the aircraft by means of the stick, thereby achieving the height control effect. The desired aileron effect is achieved by tilting to the left or right (stick movement in the same direction). The foot control operates the rudder in the usual way as with normal aircraft.

Manual control The manual control is structured as follows:
The stick tube is in the stick shoe, which rests on ball bearings in the stick bearing in the longitudinal direction of the aircraft (pulling - pushing).

The stick bearing itself is rotatably mounted in the transverse direction on ball bearings (transverse control) on the longitudinal tube of the fuselage.

A bumper leads from the stick shoe to the angle lever mounted on the head support and from there another bumper on the head support to the height control lever, which carries the rotary vane axis.

The bumpers are adjustable in length and equipped with self-aligning ball bearings. The bumper connected to the stick also has an additional bearing that allows the rod heads to be rotated against each other when the steering wheel is deflected.

The transverse control is transferred from the stick to the head by means of an endless cable with turnbuckles. It is attached to the stick bearing with a clamping screw. From here it leads over two rope segments and a pair of rope pulleys on the longitudinal tube and another on the folding axis of the head support into the head support and from there over a guide pulley to the transverse control lever on the transverse control shaft, to which it is fastened again with clamping screws.

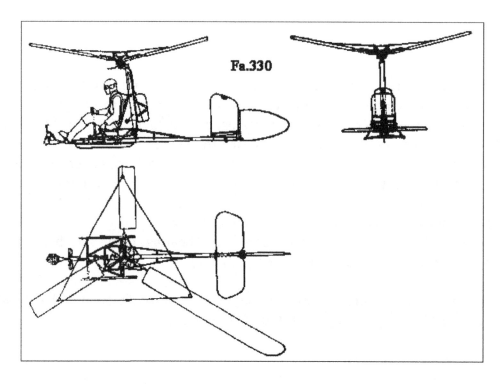

Foot control

The foot control consists of the control log mounted on the longitudinal tube, two cables that are guided into and out of the longitudinal tube through synthetic resin guide pieces, and the side control lever, which is mounted at the end of the longitudinal tube. From this, the deflections of the steering wheel are transferred to the rudder through pins in the rudder lever. When driving, the rudder is coupled to the tail (see land landing gear, tail).

5. Structure

The supporting structure consists of the rotary wing bracket, the rotary wing head and three rotary wing leaves.

Rotary wing bracket

The rotating sash bracket consists of the head carrier and the V-shaped head carrier support.
The head support is a thin-walled steel tube with a large diameter, which is pivotably mounted on the longitudinal tube of the fuselage.

The support supports the head carrier to the front of the fuselage frame, on which it is also pivotably mounted. It also supports the backrest. Beam and support are connected to each other by a double snap.

At the upper end of the head support, both in the operational and in the folded state, the Quersteuerwelde is mounted, which carries the height control axis at the front. The height control lever on which the rotary vane axis (rotor axis) is located rotates on the height control axis.

Rotary wing head

The rotary wing head essentially consists of the axle bushing, the hub and three spacers. The axle socket and axle are connected to one another by a separation point. By operating an emergency release lever, the rotary wing is separated from the rotary wing bracket and thrown off at this point. The hub is mounted on the axle bush with ball bearings. The spacers are attached to the flapping hinge on the hub.

Above it, the arms lie with the stops facing upwards (rubber buffers) and downwards (hanging ropes). The flyweight ropes are connected to the suspension ropes and keep the leaves "in the star" when this is not caused by the centrifugal force.

On the lower part of the hub, the pulley for turning the rotary vane is mounted on a freewheel. The brake shoes for the Roterbremse are located inside the pulley.

There is a ring gear on the lower part of the hub to take the speed measurement.

The intermediate pieces have a horizontal axis (flapping hinge) on the inside and a vertical axis (swivel joint) on the outside, thus enabling the rotating blades to move in both directions at the same time. A friction damper is attached to each intermediate piece, which dampens the movements of the blade around the pivot axis via a bumper. It consists of an upper and a lower part of the housing and carries the metal washers, intermediate layers and a rubber washer inside, which generate the braking effect when the bumper is actuated.

Rotary vane blades

The single rotary leaf consists of a tubular steel spar, plywood ribs, plywood nose and covering and is connected to the intermediate piece by a quick-release fastener in the swivel joint. The quick-release fastener is formed by a pull-out but not releasable bolt, the surface of which does not serve as a running surface during pivoting movements. Between the connecting fork and the first rib, the spar carries the catch for the damper bumper, and further up the catch connection for the flyweight ropes.

6. General equipment

The following devices are built into the device board, which is detachably attached to the front of the fuselage:
An airspeed indicator for low airspeeds with a measuring nozzle or pitot tube.
A tachometer . The speed meter is connected by a two-wire line to the electric speed sensor, which is attached to the height control axle and is driven by the ring gear on the rotary wing head via a pinion.

Other devices:

The launch system
The "ground equipment for Fa 330" is intended for flight operations and to accommodate the gyroplane tow aircraft Fa 330. They consist of the launch system and the equipment for accommodation,

In the case of chassis applications , the starting system consists of the towing winch with tow rope, the starter rope and the floor communication units .

In the case of a start-up charter application , the start-up system consists of the following parts

A. Start table

1. General lake use
The take-off table is a grating that is used to store and secure the aircraft during take-off and landing. It can be folded down at the front and is supported by two spring struts at the rear. The leading edge is covered with rubber at the top so that the aircraft can be held firmly by friction when it is lashed in place. The rear end of the take-off table is formed by a steel tube mounted in rubber, which allows the aircraft, which is tilted backwards during take-off, to slide sideways, so that the pilot gets the feeling for the correct aileron deflection when taking off. Two hemp ropes, which are knotted nearby, are used to cover the cleats on the starting sled runners. On the front edge of the table below the rubber pad there are two additional cleats to be able to cover the front ends of the runners.

2. Submarine usage
In the case of submarine use, the above applies, only the start table is arranged behind the two storage containers, on each of which a support arm for holding the start table is welded (see start system for submarine use).

B. caster

For general sea and submarine use, there is a swivel pulley several meters from the launch table, over which the tow rope leads from the winch to the aircraft. In order to enable the rope to be inserted and removed quickly, the swivel roller is fastened with quick-release fasteners and is arranged in such a way that it can yield to any direction in which the cable is pulled.

The increasing angle of the rope from the swivel roller to the aircraft standing on the take-off table must not be less than 10 ° or more than 20 °. In the front part of the swivel castor block there is a bracket to facilitate the assembly of the fuselage.

The Allies came into possession of an Fa 330 in May 1944 when they captured the U-852 intact. After the war, the British government did successful experiments towing Fa 330s behind ships and jeeps, but the development of the helicopter quickly occupied the attention of the military

C. Towing winch

1. General information for sea and submarine use
The aircraft is towed by a telephone tow rope that is wound on a tow winch.
A shoe brake enables the aircraft to be released gently, held at any rope length and pulled in to the take-off position. In order to have a control over the missed rope length, marks in the form of 5 cm wide yellow colored rings are attached over the entire rope length (50 m = 1 ring; 100 m = 2 rings; 150 m = 3 rings etc.). Distance from ring to ring 5 cm.

2. Submarine usage

The winch is equipped with a 10 HP compressed air motor for submarine use . If the motor fails, a hand crank is available that is attached to the winch. A hand wheel on the left side of the winch operates a brake, with the help of which one can regulate the release and hold the desired rope length. A compressed air valve, which is attached to the winch, is used to regulate the pull-in process.

The winch with motor is housed in a pressure vessel with a collar ring cover closure. The lid of the pressure vessel must be open during operation. On top of the pressure vessel there is a bracket to support the fuselage during assembly.

In an emergency, the rope can be cut by a cutting device. When removing the winch, the motor is dismantled separately.

U-boats that deployed Fa 330 kites included at least U-177, U-181, and U-852. Otto Giese wrote, "Our boat was rigged with a Bachstelze. This was a small, single, piloted helicopter attached to a long steel cable and lifted into the air by the speed of the boat while the cable was gradually reeled out. From his position aloft, the pilot had a 360-degree view and could report any vessels.

D. Intercom

For both purposes of use, a total of three intercom stations were provided for permanent voice communication between the aircraft and the vehicle , which are distributed among the pilot, the man at the winch and the commanding officer. The latter two connections are on the winch. The voice connection is made from the winch via the telephony tow rope, which is terminated at both ends with a cable head, to a junction box attached to the aircraft.

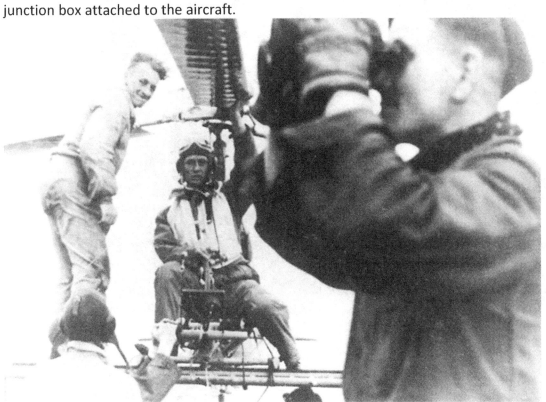

Note the winch operator and pilot with leather helmets with headphones

E. Starting coil

The turning rope, which is wound onto the turning reel, is used to turn the rotary vane. In both types of use, the spool is mounted on the front right at a fixed point. The crank of the start-up reel is set up so that it can be removed if necessary.

When not in use, the Fa 330 was stowed in two watertight compartments aft of the conning tower

Recovering, dismantling, and stowing the Fa 330 took approximately 20 minutes and was a difficult operation

Flettner Fl 185

Year   1932
Main rotor diameter   12.00 m
Length 5.80 m
Height 2.70 m
Empty weight 700 kg
Maximum takeoff weight   9000 kg
Engine 1 BMW-Bramo Sh 14A
Power 1 x 150 HP
Crew   1

Flettner built a two-seat Flettner Fl 184 autogyro with a three-bladed auto-rotating rotor and power provided by a 104kW Siemens-Halske Sh 14 radial engine driving a tractor propeller. This, was destroyed before it could be evaluated and the prototype Fl 185 followed, this being a combined autogyro/helicopter. Its Siemens-Halske engine, mounted at the fuselage nose, could be used to drive two variable-pitch propellers mounted on outriggers, one on each side of the fuselage, but the main rotor was powered only when required for operation in a helicopter mode. When flown as an autogyro the propellers on the out-riggers were both set to act as pushers and the main rotor auto-rotated. For helicopter flight the main rotor was powered from the engine and the outrigger propellers set so that one acted as a tractor and the other as a pusher to offset rotor torque.

This aircraft was a single-seater of the autogyro type with a Siemens-Halske engine. The rotor had cyclic pitch control. In the course of its tests the Fl 184 caught fire and was completely destroyed. The engine was a Siemens-Halske 14 rated 140hp, and had a rotor diameter of 12m

This convertible type aircraft, besides its three-bladed lifting rotor, had two variable-pitch airscrews mounted on either side on lateral outriggers, with thrust in opposite directions to counteract rotor torque.

The engine, situated in the nose, was cooled by a three-bladed adjustable fan consuming about 14hp, and in horizontal flight the remaining power was used to drive the outboard airscrews while the lifting rotor revolved by auto-rotation. The main gearbox was in the front part of the cockpit.

The Fl.185, which had a three-wheeled undercarriage, was given only a few tests near the ground, and then abandoned in favour of the Fl.265, which embodied the intermeshing rotor system on which Flettner had now begun to work.

The Fl 185 was only flown a few times before Flettner began construction, in 1937, of his Fl 265 VI prototype (D-EFLV), first flown in May 1939. This was of similar airframe configuration to the Fl 185, but dispensed with the outriggers and propellers, and introduced two two-bladed counter-rotating inter-meshing and synchronised main rotors which, because they were rotating in opposite directions, each cancelled the effects of the other's torque. To simplify control problems a tail unit incorporated an adjustable tailplane for trimming purposes, and for steering a large fin and rudder to augment the use of differential collective-pitch change on the two rotors. The aircraft was lost in an accident some three months later when the counter-rotating blades struck each other, but the Fl 265V2 was used successfully for a variety of military trials. In all, six prototypes were built under contract to the German navy before, in 1940, an order was placed for quantity production. By then, however, Flettner had de signed a more advanced two-seat helicopter and it was decided instead to proceed with the development and manufacture of this improved aircraft.

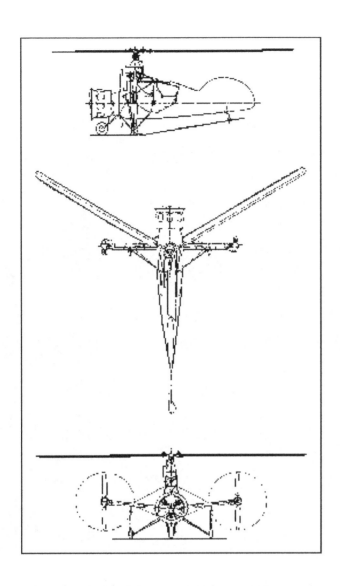

Flettner Fl 265

In 1937 Flettner began to design the first helicopter to use intermeshing contra-rotating synchronized rotors. The following year the German Navy gave Flettner an order for six of these single-seater helicopters, powered by a 7-cylinder air-cooled engine to drive its two intermeshing two-bladed rotors and with an inertia damping system to reduce the shake of the control stick.

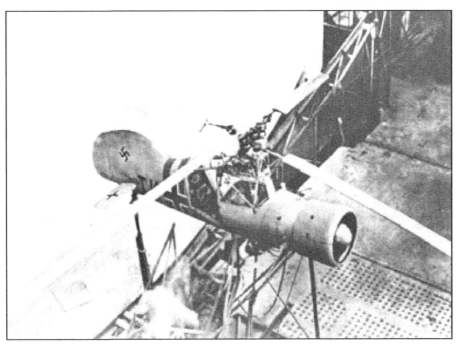
Windtunnel test of a Fl 265

Interestingly, the Fl 265 wasn't actually conceived for use with the German Luftwaffe (Air Force) but rather it was for the Kriegsmarine (Navy), which sought to create a vertical takeoff/landing craft that could be used on ships as the German military lacked a conventional aircraft carrier.

The reasoning of that the Luftwaffe was the contractor behind helicopters, was that all aircraft and development of aircraft was under the command of the Luftwaffe by order of Hermann Göring. This also hampered the development of the German Aircraft carriers, because the Luftwaffe would have the last say in development of carrier based aircraft.

The Kriegsmarine concluded that it would be necessary to develop three helicopters - one for use from a shore base, a compact shipboard model and a mini-version that could potentially be carried on submarines for scouting operations.

Year   1939
Main rotor diameter   12.30 m
Length 6.16 m
Height 2.82 m
Empty weight 800 kg
Maximum takeoff weight   1000 kg
Engine 1 BMW-Bramo Sh 14A
Power 1 x 160 HP
Maximum speed   150 km/h
Cruising speed 135 km/h
Practical range 300 km
Service ceiling 4100 m
Crew   1

Demonstration of the Flettner Fl 265, attending Ernst Udet and Anton Flettner the designer

This resulted in the development of the experimental Fl 265. One of the aircraft that was to fulfill the Kriegsmarines needs was the brainchild of Anton Flettner, a German aviator and engineer who worked for Count Zeppelin during World War I. In total, six prototypes of Flettner's design were ordered for testing.

The thinking was these small, one-manned aircraft could be launched from surface ships or specially-modified U-Boats and provide an "eye-in-the-sky" that was at the time nearly unavailable to the German Navy. The Fl 265 first flight took place in May 1939. During this flight the blades struck each other and the helicopter was destroyed. A similar fate overtook the second one, because the pilot had for-gotten to fill his fuel tanks. The remaining four Fl 265s in the original contract were extensively tested on the deck of the German cruiser Köln (Cologne) with such encouraging results that work was speeded up on the development ot the Fl 282, a second intermeshing rotor helicopter to embody the experience acquired during the tests of the Fl 265.

Flight testing of the Fl 265 on the light cruiser Köln (Cologne)

Fl 265 airborne of the German light cruiser Köln(Cologne)

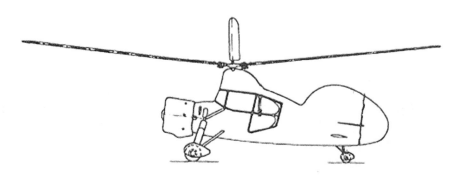

Flettner Fl 265

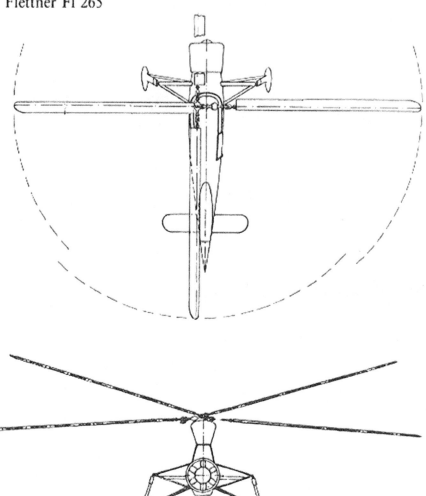

Top view of the inter meshing rotors

Flettner 282 KOLIBRI

Flettner Fl 282V-2 with its glass nose

The pioneer work of Anton Flettner is often overshadowed by the more publicised activities of his contemporaries Focke and Sikorsky; yet Flettner's first fully practical helicopter, the Fl 265, was far superior to the Fw 61 and made a successful free flight several months before the VS-300 began tethered flights. Flettner's first rotorcraft, flown in 1932, had a 2-blade rotor 29.87m in diameter, with a 30hp Anzani engine mounted part of the way along each blade driving a propeller, a form of propulsion similar to that used by the Italian Vittorio Isacco on his so-called 'helicogyros' developed in the U.S.S.R. in the 1930s. The Flettner machine made a successful tethered take-off, but later overturned during a gale and was written off. His next significant design was the Fl 184 single-seat autogyro; powered by a 150hp Sh.14 radial engine, it flew in 1935 and was due to be evaluated by the German Navy when it, too, was unfortunately destroyed. The next design was the Fl 185, whose prototype (D-EFLT) flew in 1936 and had a 3-blade main rotor. The centrally-mounted Sh.14A engine drove, in addition to the rotor, two small anti-torque propellers on outriggers each side of the cabin and a large cooling fan in the nose.

The idea of the helicopter was new at that time and Anton Flettner and his team made a lot of efforts to convince the German Air Ministry that they had a good product. One of these efforts was to take an average German housewife and teach her to fly the new helicopter

They finally proved that the vehicle was extremely stable and very easy to fly. So easy, that an average German housewife with no previous flying experience, managed to control the Fl 282V22 helicopter, after only 3 hours of flight training

The fuselage was constructed from truss-type welded steel tube, covered with doped fabric. It was fitted with a fixed non-retractable tricycle type undercarriage, with the braced fixed nose wheel with VDM oil shock absorber leg coupled with the rudder foot pedals for steering. Nose wheel was equipped with a 350x150 mm tire and main gear with 465x165 mm tires. The rectangular outline with rounded tips rotor blades were made by tubular steel spar with riveted-on wooden ribs and plywood skin with fabric covering and axes of both rotors were angled outboard at 12° from the vertical. Seen from above, the right rotor rotates clockwise and the left rotor counter clockwise. At the rear end of the fuselage, a two-part horizontal stabilizer with single spar was provided for trimming purposes and a rudder fin of very generous area. This large area was necessary because much of it was ineffective due to the poor aerodynamic shape of the fuselage causing rearwards flow separation and turbulence. It was constructed by tubular steel spar with riveted-on wooden ribs, plywood leading edge & fabric-covered. Steering of the Fl 282 was by a combination of the rudder and differential collective pitch change on the two rotors, but only the rudder could give steering during autorotation since collective pitch was then ineffective (another reason for the large rudder area). Rudder fin was made of wood and covered by fabric, with 40° deflection. The vertical stabilizer and the elevators were also made of wood, with plywood leading edge and fabric covering, bolted to fuselage frame.

Again the Fl 282V-2, showing its a glass canopy

Flettner Fl282V-3

Extremely manoeuvrable and very stable, even in gusty conditions, the machine could be flown hands-off in forward flight above 60 km/h for indefinite periods by making an adjustment to neutralize the loads on the controls. However, in forward flight at speeds below 60 km/h there was some longitudinal instability, which reached a maximum at about 40km/h. Another slight criticism of the Fl 282 was that it vibrated rather badly while the rotor was running up on the ground, but this vibration decreased upon lifting off, although there was still a certain amount of vibration transmitted to the control column, which was sluggish and tended to overshoot the requisite amount of movement. Although many of the mechanical components were unnecessarily complicated and heavy, the general design and workmanship were of excellent quality.

Dashboard of the Flettner Fl 282

The two two-blade rotors, which were synchronized to be parallel in the 45° position, were mounted on shafts having an included angle of 24° between them and an inclination forward of 6°. The rotor blades consisted of wooden ribs mounted on tubular steel spars with a covering of plywood followed by fabric. Flapping and dragging hinges were fitted, the latter having friction dampers. A centrifugally-operated blade-pitch governor held the rotor rpm within prescribed limits, the governor being driven through clutches from the rotor transmission. In order to ensure that power-off autorotation was not lost, the governor was set for a minimum rotor speed of 160 rpm. With the use of his collective-pitch lever, the pilot could over-ride the governor but only to increase rpm. Under certain conditions, self-excited oscillations could occur in the rotor; this pheno menon happened in flight on one occasion when an Fl 282 was being flown with a high collective pitch and the low rotor speed of 140 rpm (compared with the recommended 175 rpm). Vibration became so severe that the pilot prepared to bale out, but, before he could do so, the machine went into autorotation and the vibration ceased.

At the rear end of the fuselage, a horizontal stabilizer was provided for trimming purposes and a fin and rudder of very generous area. This large area was necessary because much of it was ineffective due to the poor aerodynamic shape of the fuselage causing rearwards flow separation and turbulence. Steering of the Fl 282 was by a combination of the rudder and differential collective pitch change on the two rotors, but only the rudder could give steering during autorotation since collective pitch was then ineffective (another reason for the large rudder area).

61

Taxiing under its own power was strictly forbidden, this rule was imposed because the non vertical angled rotor hubs resulted in the blade tips at the sides of the craft being around human body height and made the craft dangerous to approach from the ground whilst the blades were spinning. In addition, the blades could be damage by contact with the ground. At heliports these two problems could be overcome, but at unprotected sites this would be a concern. So, they had a simple rule that ground crew could not approach at that time or only directly from the front.

Fl 282V12 registered as CJ-SF, pushed back by ground personnel

The Fl 282 was more highly developed and flew more hours than any other German helicopter, and very extensive tests and measurements were made of all flight aspects. Most of this test work was done by Flettner's chief pilot, Hans E. Fuisting, who also undertook blind flying and trained many of the 50 pilots who learned to fly the Fl 282. Some new pilots ran into trouble when flying near the ground, because, as they turned with the wind, they lost lift and struck the ground. One new pilot had a fatal accident when flying his Fl 282 blind in cloud, and the assumed cause of the accident was that the machine had been dived and the controls then pulled back so violently that the blades were forced into each other or into the tail. The diving speed thereafter was restricted to 175km/h. On occasions, the Kolibri was landed autogyro fashion and without the use of collective pitch. This was done by descending vertically, diving nose-down and then pulling back on the controls to land, but, on one occasion at least, the tail hit the ground and was damaged.

The Kriegsmarine HQs was impressed with the Flettner Fl-282 Kolibri and wanted to evaluate it for submarine spotting duties, ordering an initial 15 helicopters, to be followed by 30 production models. Flight testing of the first two prototypes (with enclosed plexiglass panelled cabins and 3-bladed rotors installed, instead of the 2-bladed rotors on production models) was carried out through 1941, including repeated takeoffs and landings from a 13 m² wide platform pad mounted on the German cruiser Köln(Cologne). Intended roles of Flettner Fl 282 Kolibri included ferrying items between Kriegsmarine ships and naval reconnaissance operation from cruisers and other warships. The entire Fl 282 flight test program was not conducted at Rechlin, as was customary for land based aircraft; instead, from August 1942, trials were carried out at E-Stelle See Travemünde. Travemünde was selected because the air traffic safety ship Greif was based there and could be used for deck landing trials. The site also simplified helicopter sea trials with the navy, it was also imperative to move the site of the trials from Flettner's facility in Berlin, where there was a greater risk from the growing Allied bombing raids.

Hans E. Fuisting performed most of the Fl 282 test-flying

On September 1942 a Fl 282V12 Kolibri with registration CJ-SF, was initially tested by Anton Flettner's chief pilot Oberleutnant (1st Lieutenant) Hans E. Fuisting, aboard the Kriegsmarine's ship Greif, a 2000 ton aircraft salvage ship. Few weeks later, in October 1942, another two Fl-282 helicopters, one V6 version with registration GF-YF and one V10 version with CJ-SD registration, were delivered to Trieste with their personnel, including Hauptmann (Captain) Klaus von Winterfeldt, Anton Flettner's chief pilot Oberleutnant (1st Lieutenant) Hans E. Fuisting and a 3rd pilot (his name & rank are unknown) plus three mechanics for technical support. From November 1942 until February 1943, the Fl 282V6 registered as GF-YF, had been extensively tested aboard the Kriegsmarine's Flugzeugbergungsschiff "Drache" (Aircraft rescue ship, "Schiff 50", ex-Yugoslavian "Zmaj") while operating in Aegean Sea, north of Crete, Greece, following the absence of RAF aircrafts in the area for few months. The second V10 Kolibri registered as CJ-SD, was a reserve machine that stayed ashore.

The helicopter was operated from a 15 m² wide platform pad, while the ship was moving. It was no simple matter setting a helicopter down on the waving deck of a ship, so a special system was designed to bring the two vehicles together. A 10 meters long cable was attached to a swiveling fixture on the bottom of the helicopter. The pilot would bring the helicopter in to hover just out of ground effect over the platform and release the free end of the cable. Two men on the deck would grab the cable and hook it onto the winch drum, pulling the helicopter down to the deck. While this was going on the pilot applied enough power to keep the cable taunt, thus the helicopter took the waves in unison with the ship. The reverse procedure would be performed for take-off. A similar method is still used today for operating helicopters off of ships in rough weather.

By 1943, the Fl 282s were routinely being used by the Kriegsmarine for convoy protection and reconnaissance. Usually they flew from platforms above the gun turrets of convoy escort vessels in the Aegean, Baltic and Mediterranean Seas, often in extreme weather conditions. The Flettner Fl 282s revealed control and performance qualities well above expectations and found to be especially valuable at dawn or dusk when fixed wing aircraft pilots did not have good visual contact in the poor light. As an important area of operations, the Mediterranean Sea offered the promise of worthwhile missions for the Kolibri and the tactical trials could be conducted into the most favourable weather conditions. As well, the U-617 submarine was also available to participate to the trials. During the day, helicopter crews could spot the submarine as deep as 130 ft. Once a sub was spotted the Kolibri could easily match the speed & course of the submarine, which was impossible for the fixed wing aircraft with stall speeds higher than the cruise speed of a submarine. The Fl 282 would then radio transmit the sub's position to the convoy and if a warship was dispatched to attack on sub, the helicopter would mark the target's position with a magnesium flash bomb or marker flares. The V9 helicopter registered as CJ-SC was the prototype for a version to be operated by the Navy from large submarines and designated as Fl 282 U (Umbau) "Modified Model in Form of a Standing Cylinder" version. Although the Fl 282 was designed so the rotor blades and landing gear could be removed and the helicopter stored in a compact area such as the pressure tank of a U-boat, there is no evidence that it was ever used this way.

Fl 282V6, with a landing light mounted under the instrumental panel

Further service trials carried out later in the Baltic Sea aboard the anti-submarine vessel KUJ 13 (type KUJ 41) from 24th April 1943 to 15th May 1943, in conjunction with the 21st U-boat training flotilla, as part of the Kriegsmarine's ongoing exercises for sea missions in the area of Danzig Bay and the north tip of Gotland island. The fleet exercises involved underwater attacks on simulated convoys consisting of target vessels & escorts. Once, over a convoy, test pilot Hauptmann (Luftwaffe Captain) Klaus von Winterfeldt was able to make out all twelve submarines that sent against convoy.

On May 3rd and 4th 1943, a special experiment took place in cooperation with the DVL's Institute for Marine Aviation. It involved 'towing tests with a 50 kg gliding body". The proposal originated from Hauptmann (Captain) Klaus von Winterfeldt, director of the Erprobungs und Lehrkommando (Testing and Instruction Detachment) that time, who carried out the towing flights from an anti-submarine vessel in Gotenhafen. In addition to its role as a reconnaissance aircraft in support of the sub-chasers, armed with bombs the Fl 282 was also to participate actively in the anti-submarine role. Unfortunately, on May 10th 1943, Hauptmann (Captain) Klaus von Winterfeldt ran out of fuel, and crashed into the sea (35 nm NE from Christlansoya island) and killed, while flown the GF-YF registered V6 testing helicopter. He was posthumously promoted to Luftwaffe Major for his work in helicopter development.

Hauptmann (Captain) Klaus von Winterfeldt

As the War progressed, the Luftwaffe began considering converting the Kolibri for battlefield use. Until this time the helicopter had been flown by a single pilot, but by then a seat for an observer was added at the very rear of the craft, resulting in the V21 and later the V23 reconnaissance liaison versions with two seats for pilot and observer. These helicopters later proved a useful tool on multiple roles, used for picking up downed airmen, artillery spotting and other observation duties. It was similar to the naval helicopter, but a rearwards facing seat for the observer was positioned behind the rotor shafts. This made necessary the removal of the main fuselage fuel tank with consumable content 105 litres of 87-octane aviation gasoline. The standard fuel tank was removed and replaced by two un-protected, 25 litres cylindrical fuel tanks mounted externally on both sides of the pilot seat. The FuG 19 ultra short wave radio installation of the naval version was also replaced with a smaller and lighter short range radio. The naval version's one-man inflatable raft, the single-barrel flare pistol, the hand operated signal lamp and other sea survival equipment were also removed. Beginning in 1944, the Luftwaffe began to implement a program to provide a helicopter to each Wehrmacht's independent artillery brigade.

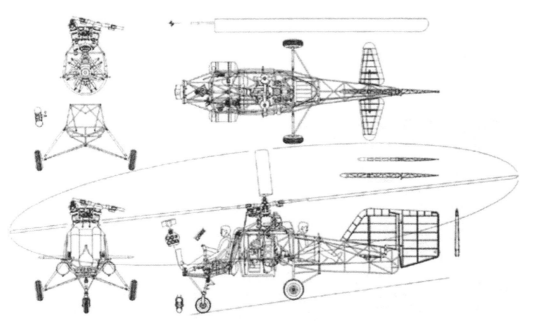

One Fl 282 accumulated 95 flying hours without any repairs

The twin seat Fl-282 V21 helicopter registered as CI-TU, as seen while been tested with two men in rear compartment plus pilot. Anton Flettner himself took part on these test flights sitting in the rear observer's seat and company chief pilot Oberleutnant (1st Lieutenant) Hans E. Fuisting on the flight controls.

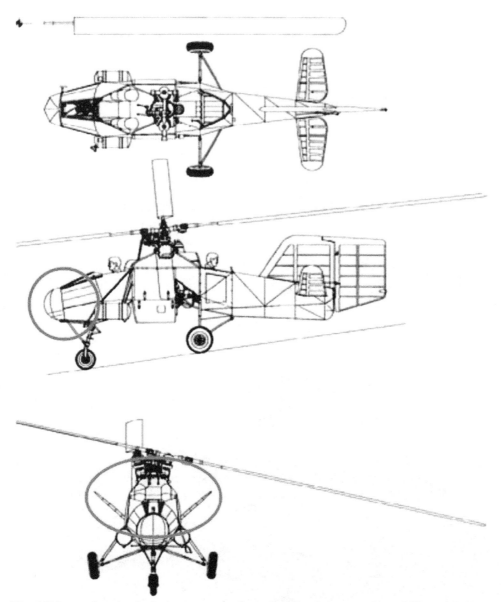

The V23 version had also two seats for pilot & observer, but differed from V21 because it was equipped with V-shaped stabilizer (similar to that of the Cierva C-30) and also had wooden cockpit sidewalls, as visible on the diagram above

On June 22nd 1944 a mock combat between the Fl 282V12 (registered as CJ-SF) with chief pilot Oberleutnant (1st Lieutenant) Hans E. Fuisting on the controls and a FW-190 with pilot Oberleutnant (1st Lieutenant) Dieter Eisenlohr of Erprobungskommando (Testing Command) EKdo 25, took place at Schweidnitz, in order to investigate the chances of a fighter hitting a helicopter. A camera was installed in the wing of the Focke-Wulf Fw 190 fighter, with the shutter release connected to the firing button. The combat was scheduled to last twenty minutes. During the first ten minutes, combat had to take place at altitudes above 330 ft (100 m). For the final ten minutes Kolibri's pilot Hans E. Fuisting was advised that he could do as he wished. Camera film evaluation and both pilot written reports revealed that at altitudes more than 100 meters AGL (Above Ground Level) the fighter was able to get the helicopter in gun sights briefly but when near the ground, especially in difficult terrain, the fighter had little chance against a helicopter. The Fw 190 pilot tried very hard and made the steepest possible turns to keep the helicopter into his gun sights. On the other hand, the Fl 282 helicopter pilot, only made slight evasive movements up, down or sideways so that he could escape from being into Fw 190 gun sights. During the second part of the combat exercise, the Fl 282 helicopter simply vanished from the fighter, partly hidden between the trees as Hans E. Fuisting showed his mastery of nap-of-the-earth flying. Fw 190's pilot Oberleutnant (1st Lieutenant) Dieter Eisenlohr's recollection of events is similar: "...At altitude above 330 ft (100 m) the Fl 282 seemed a small target clearly visible against the blue sky and I could partly compensate for Fuisting's evasive movements but during the second part of our combat, I had great difficulty spotting him in the meadows and forests around Schweidnitz. I twice spotted the Fl-282's because sunlight reflection on rotating blades & flat plexiglass panels of cabin and I had to make a 180° tight turn to try and get it in my gun sights..." The June 1944 Monatsbericht (monthly report) of E-Stelle Travemunde noted: "...At present time, the evaluation of the film and the pilot reports have not arrived yet. At heights above 100 m the fighter was able to get the helicopter in its sights briefly. Near the ground, especially in difficult terrain, the fighter has little chance against a helicopter...".

The Fl 282V12 with partial plexiglass enclosure of the cockpit, as used on the June 22nd 1944 mock combat against a Fw 190 fighter

Vulnerability to gunfire was also investigated, whereby they proceeded on the assumption that the mathematical probability of a moving rotor blade being hit was much less than that of a fixed wing. Another consideration was that the helicopter could escape by making brief evasive movements, which the fighter could not follow. Furthermore, tests involving ground firing at the moving rotor blades were carried out, as the helicopter was felt to be more vulnerable to gunfire from the ground than from the air. An unmanned, tethered Kolibri was used; in spite of several hits in the rotor blades ground fire failed to bring down the helicopter.

Fl 282V17, following a crash landing at Travemünde

Good flight characteristics and easy handling in bad weather, led the German Air Ministry to issue a contract being given in 1944 to the BMW - Bayerische MotorenWerke for 1000 helicopters production. However, the factories based in Munich and Eisenach was completely destroyed by the Allied bombing raids. The Flettner Johannisthal factory was also bombed and by the end of the War, this concern had completed only 24 operational helicopters (10 helicopters before 1943 plus 14 helicopters during 1943 & 1944). Due to the growing number of Allied air raids on Berlin, in August 1943 the company began transferring its operations to Schweidnitz in Silesia (approx. 50 km SW of Breslau); due to the deterioration of the transportation system the operation took several months. The Fl 282s on hand with the company were also flown to Schweidnitz to continue the test program. In February 1944 the workforce reached approximately 120 men, its highest level ever. With the Red Army approaching Silesia, the company moved back to Berlin Tempelhof in January and February 1945. Any systematic work or further production was of course out of the question under these circumstances. To make matters worse, two days after its arrival the rest of the company's equipment was destroyed in a night raid on Tempelhof. What was left of Anton Flettner Flugzeugbau GmbH was subsequently evacuated to Bad Tölz (Upper Bavaria); two Fl 282s were also flown there. The story Anton Flettner Flugzeugbau GmbH ended there with the arrival of US Army troops.

Towards the end of World War II, most of the surviving Flettner Fl 282s were stationed at Rangsdorf and Ainring at Mühldorf, Bavaria, in their role as artillery spotters, assigned to TransportStaffel (transport squadron) 40, the Luftwaffe's only operational helicopter squadron but gradually fell victim to Soviet fighters and anti-aircraft fire. During the last few months of the War the Luftwaffe's Transport Staffel 40 squadron made many flights into and out of besieged and encircled towns transporting dispatches, mail and key personnel. It was possibly one of this unit's Fl 282s that flew Gauleiter (governor of Lower Silesia, Bavaria), Reichsführer SS and Chief of the Deutsche Polizei Karl August Hanke, to his escape out of besieged Breslau, on May 5th 1945, letting him escape to Prague, just one day before the capture of that city. It seems that it was a Fl 282V21, as the only available two-seater helicopter in squadron that date, since the other V23 two-seater, had been flown away and hidden at Bad Tölz few days earlier (on April 26th 1945 flown by company's chief pilot Hans E. Fuisting). By May 7th 1945, the Soviets were located less than 19 miles away from Fl 282 base and orders were received to transfer westward to avoid capture. On May 8th 1945, the ground element of TransportStaffel 40 set out by road to Zell-am-See. Since there were no available pilots for the remaining Fl 282s, attempts were made to destroy the helicopters. Unfortunately, very few Fl-282s survived the War and only five found by the Allies in a serviceable condition for testing and evaluating. Also unfortunately, the Fl 282 helicopter was not so much photographed and there are not available photographic records of each one of these 24 helicopters produced. Actually, the total (known) photographs while serving under Kriegsmarine's and Luftwaffe's markings, might not exceed total 100 - in which more usual protagonists are the V6 (naval tests) and the V21 (double seats), both typical examples of the type but both did not survive the War.

Photo of Fl 282 V12 with a good view of the pilot seat with harness and the rotor head. The four "pots" on the blade roots are vibration dampers

A German Flettner Fl282 during helicopter trials aboard Drache, formerly the Yugoslavian seaplane tender Zmaj

Yugoslavian seaplane tender Zmaj. A single disassembled de Havilland DH.60 Moth floatplane was stored in the aircraft hold between the forward superstructure and the mainmast. Its components would be moved from the hold by the aircraft crane to the after deck where it could be assembled. Then the aircraft would be swayed over the side where it could be launched. The aircraft was removed from the ship when she was converted into a minelayer

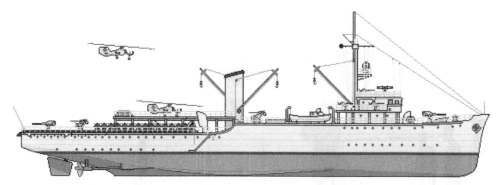

Drache, (Schiff 50, ex-Yugoslav Zmaj), Length 83m and beam 15m

Captured helicopters 1 and 2: The first two flyable helicopters were found intact by US Army troops. One V23 helicopter registered as CI-TW and one V15 registered as CJ-SI. These two Fl-282s, received the FE-4613 and FE-4614 US numbers after been captured and transported from Cherbourg Octeville, France to Newark New Jersey, USA (Operation "Seahorse" from July 12nd 1945 to July 19th 1945) aboard HMS Reaper D82 (a Bogue-class escort aircraft carrier of US Navy, leased to the Royal Navy during WWII) for further investigation. The Fl 282 V23 Kolibri was a two-seater similar to the V21, with V-shaped stabilizer fins. Into following pictures, notice the exact same V23 helicopter as seen with pre-capture Luftwaffe's CI-TW registration & swastika markings and later in USAAF service with the FE-4613 US numbers visible, after been captured.

A captured Flettner helicopter marked with FE, Foreign Equipment. Brought to USA for testing

Years   1939
Length 6.56 m
Height 2.20 m
Empty weight 760 kg
Maximum takeoff weight   1000 kg

Engine 1 BMW-Bramo Sh 14A
Power 1 x 160 HP
Cruising speed 135 km/h
Service ceiling 4100 m
Crew   2

The Flettner Fl 282 Kolibri (Hummingbird), produced by Anton Flettner of Germany

Flettner Fl 282 A marked with FE 4813, FE is the marking of USAAF meaning Foreign Equipment.

Only 24 of the 30 prototypes and 15 preproduction aircraft were completed before the war ended

The German Navy was very interested in the Flettner Fl 282. Many landings were staged on the German cruiser Köln. The Siemens-Halske Sh 14 radial engine of 150-160 hp was very reliable and only required servicing every 400 hours. This is probably trials on the Kriegsmarine ship Greif

Anton Flettner in front of a seven production Fl 282 helicopters

Fl 282 Kolibri fitted with two test seats for technical observers

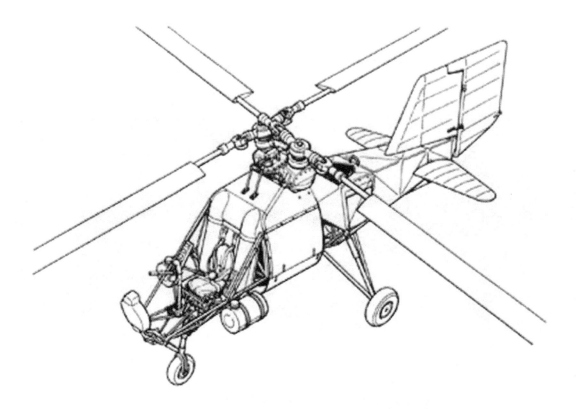

A restored Fl 282 helicopter in the U.S. around 1947. The final fate of the aircraft is unknown

A Flettner Fl 282 in Soviet markings

Captured Flettner in Soviet Russia

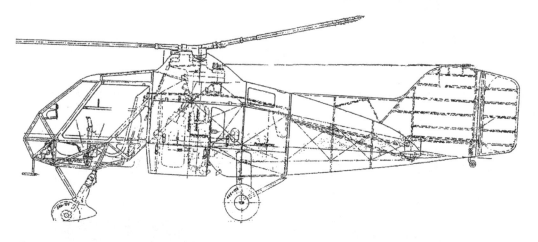

Fl 282 layout

Fl.282V-6 tethered above the platform on the deck of "Drache"

Doblhof WNF 342

Doblhof WNF342V-4

The first jet powered was the WNF 342 which was developed by Austrian Baron Friedrich von Doblhof together with Dipl. Ing. Theodor Laufer and Dipl- Ing Stephan. These where built in the austrian factory Wiener Neustadt Aircraft works..

In 1941, Friedrich von Doblhoff (1916-2000) a junior engineer at Wiener Neustädter Flugzeugwerke (Vienna-Neustadt Aircraft Factory, which assembled Bf 109 fighters,) built a static test rig on his own time from scrounged materials in order to prove his radical helicopter concept. He would eliminate the complex gearbox by spinning the rotor blades with tip-mounted jets. Factory compressed air was mixed with aviation gasoline and piped to rotor-tip combustion chambers fitted with car spark plugs.

The prototype WNF 342V1 was begun in October of 1942. It was powered by a 60hp Walter Micron engine. The operating principle was to use a conventional piston engine driving a compressor/supercharger to provide a compressed air supply, which, after mixing with fuel, was fed as a combustible mixture up through the rotor hub and out through the three hollow rotor blades to be burnt in tip-mounted combustion chambers, thereby generating thrust. Each of the first three machines (V1, V2, and V3) was provided with only a small rear propeller to blow air at the tail surfaces for steering, but the last machine (V4) had a second propeller mounted co-axially to provide thrust for forward flight when clutched to the compressor motor. Thus, by gradual development, the rotor jets (which had a high fuel consumption) were only used for take-off, hovering and landing, and the rotor blades turned by autorotation for forward flight in the manner of an autogyro. The first test was successful, so the pilot decided to risk a short hop inside the factory hall, which succeeded.

Later Luftwaffe officials were invited to witness a demonstration. With a roar and a burst of flame, the rotors whirled, and the test rig lifted off the floor. An anvil was attached to hold the prototype down. It lifted the anvil, tilted over and crashed spectacularly. The officials quickly gave von Doblhoff a development contract.

Von Doblhoff's small team built four prototypes, with a first flight in 1943. The German Navy hoped to use the craft as a light observation and anti-submarine platform (the same role as Flettner's Fl 282.) A second airframe was destroyed in a crash, and Allied bombing of the factory complex forced the team to relocate. But development work, with increasingly powerful engines, continued until the war's end.

More test models were built at workshop in Zell am See, but these were captured by Americans as they advanced into Austria. These were taken to the USA for tests.

Under the designation WNF 342, the world's first jet-driven helicopters were built by the Wiener Neustadter Flugzeugwerke (WNF) in the suburbs of Vienna, four machines being built representing progressive experimental steps in a research programme instituted in October 1942. This programme was directed by Friedrich von Doblhoff, who had decided to develop a jet-driven helicopter in preference to a mechanically-driven one because of the attraction of simplicity, lack of rotor torque and transmission gear

For the first three machines, although flapping and dragging rotor hinges were provided, no blade pitch-change arrangement was made since this was not required for early tests, vertical control being provided simply by varying the rotor speed. By the time the WNF 342V4 was built, however, a most ingenious control method had been devised to provide both collective and cyclic pitch control. Each rotor blade was connected to the rotor head by means of a flexibly coupled tube flanked by steel-strip leaf-type spring straps connected to an upper aluminium alloy casting. This upper casting rotated in a lower fixed casting, a seal being provided between the two, and fuel mixture flowed into this hollow assembly to be piped out to each blade. Passing up through the casting was a hollow fixed shaft which carried a bearing for the upper casting and which was flexibly connected to the helicopter framework. Inside this hollow shaft, a solid shaft rotated in a spherically seated bearing to carry the blade pitch control spider at its head. Thus, angular displacement of this solid shaft tilted the spider to give appropriate cyclic pitch control. For collective pitch control, the spider was connected to the solid shaft by means of a pressure regulator connected to the upper casting (containing the pressurized fuel mixture) by a pipeline. The spider was given a vertical movement according to the mixture pressure opposed by springs within the regulator. In addition, collective pitch was governed by the torsional stiffness of the centrifugally-loaded spring straps. When the pilot moved the throttle control, a rapid increase (for example) of mixture pressure and jet thrust followed by an increase in collective pitch ensued, while the rotor rpm remained constant.

The WNF 342V1 was built and first flown in the spring of 1943 but was superficially damaged the following year during an air raid on Vienna, whereupon the test programme was moved a short distance away to Obergraffendorf. Here, the 60hp Walter Mikron engine was replaced by a 90hp Walter Mikron engine, and general modifications were made to the extent that the machine was redesignated WNF 342V2.

The WNF 342V2, was built, being a somewhat heavier aircraft at 460kg gross weight, despite its open-framework fuselage. The main difference lay in the sail-like tail unit, this comprising a large single rectangular fin and an elongated rudder pivoting about a horizontal axis.

It should be emphasized that the fluid design of the WNF 342 was such that modifications, as dictated by empirical experiment, could be readily catered for. Thus, the basic framework was of all-tubular construction with no refinements, such as fairings, appearing as semi-permanent fittings until the V4 machine, although this machine was by no means intended as the final design. Starting with the V3 machine, increases were made in rotor diameter, and both the V3 and V4 used the extra power of the 140hp BMW Bramo Sh 14A engine to drive the compressor. In all designs, an Argus As 411 supercharger was adapted as a compressor. Before the end of the war, consideration was being given to replacing the compressor system with rotor mounted pulse-jets or even miniature turbo-jets.

Within their limited performance, the V1 and V2 machines flew smoothly enough, but serious vibration manifested itself in the V3 machine and eventually destroyed it. These troubles were eliminated in the last example which behaved well and was very smooth, but although it was hovered for a total of 25 hours, it was not tested in forward flight above 40 to 48km/h before the programme had to be halted. In 1945, Soviet troops approaching Vienna caused Doblhoff's team to withdraw hastily to Zell am See where the V2 and V4 machines were captured by United States' forces. The WNF 342 V4 has been preserved by the Smithsonian Institution, Washington.

Experience with the first two machines showed that the high fuel consumption of the tip-jets would make the WNF-342's operating costs prohibitive, and so a major design change was introduced in the V3 and V4 prototypes. The tip-drive system was retained for take-off, hovering and landing only, a selective clutch enabling the engine (now a 140hp Siemens-Halske Sh.14A radial) to drive a conventional pusher propeller for forward flight while the rotor blades 'free-wheeled' in autorotative pitch. To clear this propeller the rotor pylon was raised above the cabin and the tail unit was redesigned as a twin-boom assembly, that of the V3 carrying two end-plate oval fins and rudders while that of the V4 had a single fin and rudder mounted on the tailplane centre. Gross weight of the V3, a single-seater with 9.88m diameter rotors, was 548kg. The V4 had side-by-side open cockpits for a crew of two. The V3 was destroyed early in its test programme by ground resonance vibration, but the V4 had completed 25 hours of testing before, in April 1945, it was hastily taken westwards to prevent its capture by the advancing Soviet forces. It eventually fell into American hands, Doblhoff later accompanying it back to the United States to assist with further tests before joining McDonnell to work on development of the XV-1. Stepan, who had done most of the test flying on the WNF-342, joined Fairey in the United Kingdom after the war, while Laufer went to work for the SNCA du Sud-Ouest in France.

Year   1943
Type   Helicopter
Main rotor diameter   9.96 m
Length 5.07 m
Height 2.40 m
Empty weight 431 kg
Maximum takeoff weight   640 kg
Engine 1 Siemens-Halske Sh.14A
Power 1 x 140 HP
Maximum speed 48 km/h
Crew 1(2 for the V4)

Von Doblhoff's WNF 342 was originally designed as a single seat aircraft with a tubular steel frame and a fabric covered tail section. The fourth prototype added a second seat for an observer in a partially enclosed cockpit. The engine drove a compressor that fed a fuel-air mixture to the rotor hub, then through three hollow blades to tip-mounted jets. A pusher propeller behind the engine provided airflow, allowing a large rudder to control the direction of flight.

The torque problem was largely eliminated, since the rotor disc spun itself, imparting very little twist to the fuselage. The design team experimented with various tail configurations, including twin oval tail fins, before settling on a conventional single rudder.

It was found that the enormous centrifugal force at the rotor tips interfered with proper fuel-air mixing. A special heat-resistant alloy had to be found from which to fabricate the tip jets. Fuel consumption was so high that von Doblhoff decided to use the jets only for takeoff and landing. In flight WNF 342 relied on its pusher propeller, and the rotor spun freely, as with Juan De La Cierva's autogyro's principle.

By 1945 the fourth prototype had completed 25 hours of flight testing. It was captured by the Americans near Salzburg, Austria and shipped to the United States for evaluation, along with von Doblhoff himself. He enjoyed a successful postwar career in the aviation industry, helping to develop the radical experimental McDonnell XV-1.

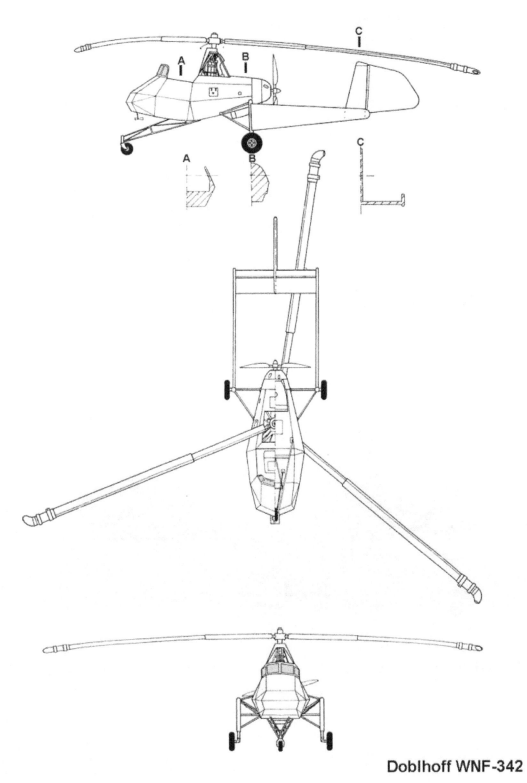

Doblhoff WNF-342

View of the light Jet helicopter WNF 342

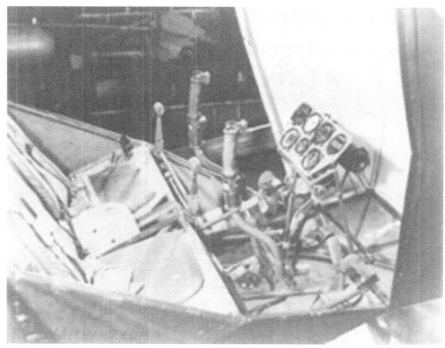

Cockpit of the Doblhof WNF 342

Doblhof WNF 342X-2

Baumgärtl Heliofly III/57

The Austrian engineer, Paul Baumgartl, concerned himself during the Second World War with the design of small single-seat helicopters, in the suburbs of Vienna. It is not certain whether his work was sponsored by the German Government, but his machines were in the same category as those of Nagler-Rolz. Baumgartl's first product was the Heliofly I of 1941, which was little more than a strap-on autogyro glider for sporting use.

Resulting from previous work was a design in 1942 for a strap-on helicopter. This was the Heliofly III-57, which had a rotor consisting of two co-axial contea-rotating single blades, each of which was to be driven by its own 8 hp Argus As 8 engine, which also acted as a counter-balance.

The Baumgärtl Heliofly III/57 and Baumgärtl Heliofly III/59 was a 1940s experimental backpack helicopters designed and built by the Austrian-designer Paul Bäumgartl. Experiments with strap-on autgyros the Heliofly III/57 was powered by two 8 hp (6 kW) Argus As 8 piston engines each driving a single-blade of the contra-rotating rotors. A problem with the supply of the As 8 engine forced a re-design to use one 16 hp (12 kW) engine, powering two rotors on a common co-axial shaft, with the engine driving one rotor directly and the other through gearing to overcome the torque effect.

A further development was called the Heliofly III/59, powered with a more powerful 16hp engine. Its dry weight was only 35kg and the takeoff weight was about 120kg. Baumgärtl had made several flights, but the desperate military situation by the end of the war put an end to his extraordinary project.

Heliofly ready for testing

Crew: 1
Length: 6.10 m (20 ft 0 in)
Empty weight: 35 kg (77 lb)
Gross weight: 120 kg (265 lb)
Powerplant: 1 × piston engine , 12 kW (16 hp)
Main rotor diameter: 2× 6.10 m (20 ft 0 in)

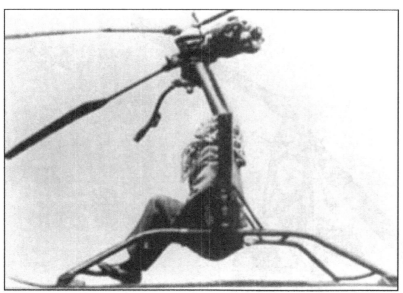

The Heliofly III-59 to be powered by a single 16 hp engine

When it became apparent that the Argus engines could not be readily obtained, the helicopter was redesigned in 1943 as the Heliofly III-59 to be powered by a single 16 hp engine. In this design, the engine drove and counterbalanced the lower blade and, through gearing, also drove the upper blade, so that torque was still counterbalanced by contra-rotation. A weight, instead of an engine, counterbalanced the upper blade, and the flapping rotor system had cyclic pitch control.

Nagler-Rolz NR 54

The Austrian Bruno Nagler began work in the rotory-wing field in 1929 when, with Raoul Hafner, he built his RI Revoplane near Vienna. This was a single seat machine with a rotor driven by a 45 hp engine and had a vertical torque-balancing surface acting in the rotor downwash. This machine, and also similar RII machine of 1932, was successfully tested in Great Britain. in 1934, Nagler brought out his Heliogyro which had a 90hp Pobjoy radial air-cooled engine, a two-blade rotor and a pusher propeller. The engine could drive the rotor for hovering, when torque was balanced by a vertical surface, or the propeller could be driven for forward flight leaving the rotor to generate lift by autorotation. This single-seat aircraft was tested in Great Britain in 1937. With the outbreak of war, Nagler joined with Franz Rolz to form the Nagler-Rolz Flugzeugbau.

The new company built a helicopter similar in configuration to the RI and RII. This ship had an empty weight of 700 pounds and though it was flown in hover, it could not be lifted out of ground effect. With the coming of World War II, the company received contacts from the German Government for the development of small single-seat helicopters.

In 1940 the first machine from the new company appeared as the NR 55, which had the unusual feature of a single-blade rotor. This rotor blade was counterbalanced by a 40hp engine which applied to it a torqueless drive by means of two small airscrews which pulled it round at about 135rpm. Because of gyroscopic forces at the engine location, the carburetor was mounted on the centerline of the rotor hub and fuel-air mixture was piped out to the engine cylinders. The rotor diameter was 10.5m, and the machine weighed about 338kg loaded, but, although a cruising speed of 97km/h was thought feasible, only hovering and lift test were undertaken because the machine was built purely for testing the rotor system.

Development of the NR 55 concept continued in 1941 with the generally similar NR 54 V1, in which considerable reductions were made in size and weight. The engine power was reduced to 24hp and the rotor diameter to 7.8m with the engines mounted 1.2m from the centerline driving the propellers, which were 1.8m further out along rotor blade. The carburetor was never perfected to work satisfactorily and due to this no test flights were ever made. Performance with empty and loaded weights of 80 and 175kg respectively, was estimated to have a 55 mph cruising speed.

The NR 54 V2 produced in 1941 was the world's first portable helicopter. By development, the simplest possible single-seat helicopter had been produced, which flew on remarkably little power. The 6.9m rotor consisted of two single blades, each of which had an 8hp motor driving a small airscrew at 6000rpm to give a torqueless drive, and the pilot's controls consisted of two levers, one to alter rotor blade pitch and the other to control the engines. The entire airframe broke down for transporting and could carried by a single man. The little ship was said to cruise at 80km/h and climb at 140m/min, not bad for only a 16 horsepower.

Four of the NR 54V2 machines were built before the war ended, but it is not known how close the NR 54 was to being ready for production at that point. At least one of them was brought to the USA for evaluation and is now in the collection of the National Air and Space Museum. The NR 54V2 is projected to be put on permanent displayed in the New Dallas Airport exhibition hall when it opens in 2000.

Nagler-Rolz NR 54
Technical data for NR 54 V2
Crew: 1, engine: 2 x 8hp, main rotor diameter: 7.92m, take-off weight: 140kg, empty weight: 36.5kg, cruising speed: 80km/h, ceiling: a457m, range: 48km

Appendix A

Hanna Reitsch

Hanna Reitsch was a leading stunt pilot before the war, she became the first woman to fly the Alps in a glider and set many other gliding records, some of which still stand today. She became chief test pilot for the Luftwaffe in 1937 and played a major role on the Junkers Ju 87 Stuka and Dornier Do 17 projects, as well as being one of the first to fly the Focke-Achgelis Fa 61, the world's first helicopter. she was the one of two women to be awarded the Iron Cross, of both first and second class.

Adolf Hitler awarding Hannah Reitsch the Iron Cross 2nd class in march 1941

Fiesler Fi 156 Storch STOL plane Reitsch used to fly to Berlin

In the last days of the war Hannah Reitsch flew into the besieged Berlin and landed in the Tiergarten near the Brandenburger Tor(Brandenburger Gate) to try to persuade and plead with Hitler to let her fly him out of Berlin to save him from the Red Army. In which she did not succeed. During the evening of 28 April, Reitsch flew von Greim out of Berlin in an Arado Ar 96 from the same improvised airstrip in the Tiergarten. This was the last plane out of Berlin. Reitsch and Von Greim escaped Berlin through heavy Russian anti-aircraft fire. Von Greim was at the time Reitsch lover, and had been appointed the Luftwaffes new commander succeding Göring, which Hitler had demoted as one of his last acts.

Two Arado Ar 96 flying formation. One of these types were used by Reitsch to escape the siege of Berlin with von Greim

She was held for 18 months in captivity by the American military after the war, she was interrogated to determine the fate Adolf Hitler and Martin Bormann. As she could not shed any new light on this she was released. When asked about being ordered to leave the Führerbunker on 28 April 1945, Reitsch and von Greim reportedly repeated the same answer: "It was the blackest day when we could not die at our Führer's side." Reitsch also said: "We should all kneel down in reverence and prayer before the altar of the Fatherland." When the interviewers asked what she meant by "Altar of the Fatherland" she answered, "Why, the Führer's bunker in Berlin ...". Von Greim killed himself on 24 May 1945.

In 1959 she was invited to India by the Indian Prime Minister Jawaharlal Nehru, where she founded a sports gliding network. Reitsch spoke fluent English, and she flew with Nehru a tour over New Delhi.

In 1961 Hanna Reitsch was invited by President John F. Kennedy to the White House, due to her female records as a aviator and as a member of the "Whirly girls"

President John F. Kennedy with members of the Association of Women Helicopter Pilots (also known as the "Whirly-Girls"). Left to right: Hanna Reitsch; Dora Dougherty; Judy Short; Ellen Gilmour; President Kennedy; Jean Wilson White House, Washington, D.C.

From 1962 to 1966, she lived in Ghana. The then Ghanaian President, Kwame Nkrumah invited Reitsch to Ghana after reading of her work in India. At Afienya she founded the first black African national gliding school, working closely with the government and the armed forces. The West German government supported her as technical adviser. She gained the FAI Diamond Badge in 1970. The project was evidently of great importance to Nkrumah and has been interpreted as part of a "modernist" development ideology.

Reitsch's attitudes to race underwent a change. "Earlier in my life, it would never have occurred to me to treat a black person as a friend or partner ..." She now experienced guilt at her earlier "presumptuousness and arrogance". She became close to Nkrumah. The details of their relationship are now unclear due to the destruction of documents, but some surviving letters are intimate in tone.

In Ghana, some Africans were disturbed by the prominence of a person with Reitsch's past, but Shirley Graham Du Bois, a noted African-American writer who had emigrated to Ghana and was friendly towards Reitsch, agreed with Nkrumah that Reitsch was extremely naive politically.

Throughout the 1970s, Reitsch broke gliding records in many categories, including the "Women's Out and Return World Record" twice, once in 1976 (715 km (444 mi)) and again, in 1979 (802 km (498 mi)), flying along the Appalachian Ridges in the United States. During this time, she also finished first in the women's section of the first world helicopter championships.

She died in 1979 of a massive heart attack at age 67. Former British test pilot and Royal Navy officer Eric Brown said he received a letter from Reitsch in early August 1979 in which she wrote, "It began in the bunker, there it shall end." Within weeks she was dead. Brown speculated that Reitsch had taken the cyanide capsule Hitler had given her in the bunker and that she had taken it as part of a suicide pact with von Greim. No autopsy was performed.

Records held by Hannah Reitsch
First woman to earn the Silver C Badge
First woman to fly a helicopter
First woman to pilot a rocket plane
First woman to fly a jet
Iron Cross First Class Luftwaffe
Pilot/Observer Badge in Gold with Diamonds (only woman)
Honorary member of the Society of Experimental Test Pilots (one of only three women)
Member #1 of the Whirly-Girls female helicopter-pilot association

1932: women's gliding endurance record (5.5 hours)
1936: women's gliding distance record (305 km (190 mi))
1937: first woman to cross the Alps in a glider
1937: the first woman in the world to be promoted to flight captain by Colonel Ernst Udet
1937: the first woman to fly a helicopter (Fa 61)
1937: world distance record in a helicopter (109 km (68 mi))
1938: the first person to fly a helicopter (Fa 61) inside an enclosed space (Deutschlandhalle)
1938: winner of German national gliding competition Sylt-Breslau Silesia
1939: women's world record in gliding for point-to-point flight.

1943: While in the Luftwaffe, the first woman to pilot a rocket plane (Messerschmitt Me 163). She survived a disastrous crash though with severe injuries and because of this she became the first of three German women to receive the Iron Cross First Class.

1944: the first woman in the world to pilot a jet aircraft at the Luftwaffe research centre at Rechlin during the trials of the Messerschmitt Me 262 and Heinkel He 162

1952: third place in the World Gliding Championships in Spain together with her team-mate Lisbeth Häfner

1955: German gliding champion

1956: German gliding distance record (370 km (230 mi))

1957: German gliding altitude record (6,848 m (22,467 ft))

Karl Bode

Karl Bode was born in Kiel/Germany on February 25, 1911. After the compulsory school he graduated as an engineer in the high technical institute of Hannover. Much later he started his activity as an airplane test pilot for various German builders. His career as a helicopter pilot started in September 1937. In that period the newly founded Focke-Achgelis company, was looking for a new test pilot. Bode accepted the offer and continued the test flights of the prototype. In 1938 inside the Deutschlandhalle of Berlin he became the first pilot to fly indoor. With this prototype he established numerous records, walloping those records precedently set. On June 20, 1938 he flew non-stop for 230 km and on January 29, 1939 he set an altitude record climbing to 3'427 meters. Despite some accidents during the tests, the success of the flights was evident. The first prototype of the Fa 223 was tested by Bode in August 1940. .

During the test flights of the new helicopter Bode was again victim of some accidents which ended fortunately without serious consequences for him.

With this helicopter he flew tests were he transported passengers, materials, light vehicles, armaments, parts of aeroplanes that had made emergency landings. The

Drache could be equipped with doubles controls and used for the training of the pilots. During the war he also flew with the small autogyro FA 330 Bachstelze towed by an U-Boot and the Focke FA 225, carrying nine soldiers.

By the end of the war the Karl Bode had logged complessively 195h18min of flight sharing out as follow: 36h 28min on the FA 61, 156h29min on the Drache and 2h13min on the Flettner Fl 282 Kolibri. At the end of the WWII the Allies prohibited almost all the flying activities in Germany. Consequently Bode was forced to cease to fly and worked as a mechanic. He then took the decision to emigrate to Switzerland where he continued his flying career.

Hans-Helmut Gerstenhauer

Hans-Helmut Gerstenhauer, born on 28th May 1915 in Diepholz (Northern Germany), grew up in Frankfurt am Oder, got first glider experience and graduated in engineering.

After the beginning of World War II, he became pilot and had flown reconnaisance aircraft (Henschel Hs 123).

After working as a test pilot at different aircraft manufacturers, he entered the company Focke , Achgelis & Co. GmbH in 1942. There he flew the unpowered autogyro Focke-Achgelis Fa 330 Bachstelze (Water wagtail) and later the helicopter Focke-Achgelis Fa 223 Drache (Dragon).

After a precarious and perilous mission in the Gdansk area in March 1945 , at which he performed the first search and rescue mission with a helicopter (rescue of a ditched Messerschmitt Bf 109 pilot), he transferred after been captured by U.S. troops the helicopter Fa 223V14 with the designation DM+SR from the Bavarian airfield Ainring to the Beaulieu airfield in southern England.

Hans-Helmut Gerstenhauer has thus undoubtedly got most flying experience on a helicopter within the period until shortly after the end of World War II and got most experience in long-distance flying on a helicopter at that time.

Hans-Helmut Gerstenhauer died on 23. October 2014.

Ewald Rohlf

Ewald Rohlfs (1911 Bremen, Germany - 1984) was a test pilot. In 1936 Rohlfs made the first flight of a helicopter, the Focke-Wulf Fw 61. One year later he took the helicopter to an altitude of 1,130 feet (344 m) and then idled the engine. using its spinning rotors to descend safely to the ground.

Henrich Focke

Focke, Henrich born in Bremen, on 8. October 1890, the son of Senate Syndicus Johann Focke (1848-1922) and his wife Louise born. Stamer. His father is the founder of the Focke Museum in Bremen. His achievements in mathematics were moderate at the elementary school as well as at the humanistic grammar school.In 1914 he volunteered as a war volunteer, but was initially withdrawn because of heart disease. Only in the fall of 1914 he was obliged to serve in the 75th Infantry Regiment. Already in the spring of

1915 he was transferred to the flying squad with the support of a friend. He studied in Hanover, where he became friends with Georg Wulf in 1911. Then in 1914, Focke and Wulf both reported for military service and Focke was deferred due to heart problems, but was eventually drafted into an infantry regiment. After serving on the Eastern front, he was transferred to the Imperial German Army Air Service. Georg Wulf's passion for flying cost him his life as he crashed during a test flight on 29-09-1927, age 32.

Focke graduated in 1920 as Dipl-Ing (MS) with distinction. His first job was with the Francke Company of Bremen as a designer of water-gas systems.

FOCKE-WULF

In 1923, with Wulf and Dr. Werner Naumann, Focke co-founded Focke-Wulf-Flugzeugbau GmbH.

In 1936 Focke was ousted from the Focke-Wulf company by shareholder pressure. Though the ostensible reason was that he was considered "politically unreliable" by the Nazi regime there is reason to believe it was so that Focke-Wulf's manufacturing capacity could be used to produce Messerschmitt Bf 109 aircraft.

The company was taken over by Aeg, but soon after this the Air Ministry, which had been impressed by the Fw 61 helicopter, suggested that Focke establish a new company dedicated to helicopter development and issued him with a requirement for an improved design capable of carrying a 700 kg (1.500 lb) payload. Focke became interested in helicopters after license production of the Cierva C. 30 autogyro.

Forty aircraft were built in Germany as the Focke-Wulf Fw 30 Heuschrecke (Grasshopper) with a 140 hp (105 kW) Siemens Sh 14A 7-cylinder radial engine.

Focke established the Focke-Achgelis company on 27. April 1937 in partnership with pilot Gerd Achgelis , and began development work at Delmenhorst in 1938.

Towards the end of the Third Reich Focke started design work on the Focke Rochen, also known as Schnellflugzeug. On 01. September 1945, Focke signed a contract with the French company SNCASE and assisted in development of their SE-3000 passenger helicopter Heinrich Focke 1890-1979 - Copy, which was based on the Focke-Achgelis Fa 223 Drache and which first flew in 1948. In 1950, he worked as a designer with the North German Automobile Company (Norddeutsche Fahrzeugwerke) of Wilhelmshaven.

Henrich Focke died highly honored and awards in Bremen on 25-02- 1979, old age 88 and is buried, with his wife Louise and son Eberhard, on the Riensberger cemetery.

Gerd Achgelis

Achgelis was born in Golzwarden in Oldenburg, and after an apprenticeship as an electrician, began working as a stunt pilot in 1928. In 1930 he flew inverted for an hour over London, and in 1931 he was the German aerobatic champion. Flying a Fw 44 Stieglitz, Achgelis was placed third in the 1934 World Aerobatic Championships in Paris, and was 5th at the 1936 event in Berlin.

From April 1932, he also worked as a flying instructor at the Technikum Weimar, and in 1933 became chief test pilot for the Focke-Wulf company in Bremen. On 26 June 1936 he flew the Focke-Wulf Fw 61, the first practical helicopter, on its maiden flight. On 27 April 1937, together with Henrich Focke, he founded the company Focke-Achgelis to develop and manufacture helicopters at Hoykenkamp.

Gerd Achgelis in front of a Focke-Wulf Kiebitz aircraft

In 1933 Hermann Göring proposed that Achgelis take a post as an instructor at the Deutsche Verkehrsfliegerschule (German Air Transport School), to establish and train an aerobatic team. Achgelis turned down the offer, and he also refused Hermann Göring's request to take the position of Generalluftzeugmeister (Luftwaffe Director-General of Equipment or in fact Quartermaster of the Luftwaffes procurement) after the death of Ernst Udet in November 1941. He worked as a test pilot at an aircraft factory in Graudenz until the end of World War II.

After the war, Achgelis retired to his family farm, and from 1952 had commercial interests in Hude. However he remained connected to flying. In 1961, he was one of the founders of the airfield Flugplatz Oldenburg-Hatten at Hatten, and in 1975, he received the légion d'honneur from France for his achievements in aviation. He also donated the Kavalier der Lüfte trophy, which is presented annually every November.

Achgelis died at his home in Hude in 1991.

Baron Friedrich von Doblhof

Baron Friedrich von Doblhoff was an Austrian helicopter pioneer.

Shortly after WW2 began, the German navy held a competition to design and build a rotary-wing aircraft to be used on small ships and submarines for scouting. Friedrich von Doblhoff proposed a helicopter with tip-jet driven rotor, and was authorised to start work with a team of engineers which included Dipl.-Ing. Theodor Laufer and Dipl.-Ing. August Stepan. Support came from Prof. Henrich Focke.

Von Doblhoff and his colleagues in front of the WNF 342

Doblhoff rotor blades were driven round by the reaction of 'hot' jets using a fuel/air mixture fed through the rotary blades using an engine-driven compressor.

The tip jets avoided the need for gearing to drive the rotor, and avoided torque reaction which would otherwise have to be counteracted by a tail propellor or by contra-rotating blades. The drawback was high fuel consumption, and this restricted the jets to take-off and landing, while in normal flight the engine would drive a pusher propeller while the rotor windmilled.

The Doblhoff WNF-342 was the first helicopter in the world to take off by the use of jets, but the end of the war curtailed the futher development by von Doblhoff. The WNF-342V4 was captured by the Allies and taken to the USA.

The jet tip concept was taken up with mixed success by a number of firms. The successful Djinn Helicopter, made in France used compressed air only (no fuel) for the tip jets. The large Fairey Rotodyne showed promise, but did not get beyond the prototype stage.

Anton Flettner

Anton Flettner (November 1, 1885 December 29, 1961) was a German aviation engineer and inventor. He made important contributions to airplane and helicopter design. He was born in Eddersheim (today a district of Hattersheim am Main).

Anton Flettner, proudly posing in front of his Fl 282s fleet at Schweidnitz (today Świdnica, Poland), on October 1944

Through a gradual process of working on various rotating-wing schemes, Anton Flettner arrived at his celebrated scheme of intermeshing rotors first employed in the Fl 265 helicopter. This scheme, though viewed with suspicion by many at the time, dominated Flettner's helicopter work a couple of years prior to, and then throughout, the war. When, in 1930, Flettner first turned his attention to helicopter problems, he designed a helicopter having a single, torqueless, rotor, the absence of torque being achieved by applying the drive directly at the rotor, two 30hp Anzani engines driving small airscrews, being attached to the rotor blades. This helicopter was unfortunately destroyed in 1933 during tethered tests when it was overturned by a gust of wind.

Flettner then turned to the design of a straightforward two-seat autogyro, the Fl 184. This machine was scheduled to carry out trials with the German Navy to ascertain its suitability for reconnaissance and anti-submarine work, such a machine offering distinct advantages over naval fixed-wing aircraft which required catapult-launching and special recovery procedures. The Fl 184 had a fully-enclosed fuselage and tail surfaces, and the 12m diameter rotor employed cyclic pitch control. At the nose was mounted a 140hp Siemens-Halske Sh 14 radial engine driving a two-blade wooden propeller. During 1936, before this design could be evaluated, the only prototype, D-EDVE, caught fire in flight and was completely destroyed.

In the next design, the Fl 185, the machine was arranged to act as a helicopter when the rotor was powered or act as an autogyro when the rotor autorotated in forward flight. A

140hp Siemens-Halske Sh 14A engine was mounted in the nose and was provided with a cowl and frontal fan for cooling. Behind the engine was a gearbox from which the drive was taken to the rotor and to two variable-pitch airscrews mounted on outrigger arms extending from the fuselage sides. When the rotor was powered, to counteract torque the airscrews provided thrust in opposite directions, but, when the rotor was freely autorotating, the pitch of the airscrews was altered to give thrust for forward flight when they also took up the full power of the engine. Again, only one prototype, D-EFLT, was built, and this was only given a few tests near the ground before being abandoned.

By this time, however, Flettner had developed the idea of counter-rotating, intermeshing twin rotors. Many of his advisers thought that the airflow disturbed by the intermeshing blades would make this system less efficient than one using a single rotor; but Flettner believed that any problems thus encountered would be more than offset by the reduced drag resulting from having no external rotor-carrying structure. He proved his point by installing such a system in the Fl 265, whose prototype (D-EFLV) flew in May 1939. At this time encouragement for the development of small helicopters came mostly from the German Navy, on whose behalf six Fl 265's had been ordered in 1938 with a view to developing a machine suitable for shipboard reconnaissance and anti-submarine patrol. Service trials of the Fl 265 were more than satisfactory, and plans were made for series production; but by this time work was well advanced on a later model, the Fl 282, which could carry a men and was more versatile. The RLM therefore agreed to wait for the Fl 282, to hasten whose development it ordered thirty prototypes and fifteen pre-production aircraft in spring 1940. Maiden flight was made in 1941. The first three prototypes were completed as single-seaters and had fully enclosed cabins made up of a series of optically flat Plexiglas panels, faired-in rotor pylons and well-contoured fuselages. The Fl 282V3 was fitted with endplate auxiliary fins and a long underfin beneath the rear fuselage. Later machines had more utilitarian bodies and some had semi-enclosed cockpits; others, like the example illustrated, had a completely open pilot's seat.

During 1938, the German Navy placed a contract for six Fl 265s, the design of which Anton Flettner had begun in 1937 as the first to use intermeshing contra-rotating synchronized rotors. The single-seat Fl 265 had a very similar fuselage and tail surfaces to the earlier Fl 185, and, once again, the engine was mounted at the nose with a cowl and cooling fan. The 160hp Bramo Sh 14A radial engine provided the power for the two two-blade rotors, which had inclined shafts mounted close together and had an inertia-damping system to reduce the vibration reaching the control column.

The Fl 265 VI, D-EFLV, made its first flight in May 1939, and its first autorotative descents were made the following August, but this machine was eventually destroyed in flight when the rotor blades struck each other. Because of this accident, the Fl 265 V2 was the first to be used in a series of naval trials in the Baltic and Mediterranean in which Fl 265s operated from platforms fitted to cruisers and even made landings on U-boat decks. Despite the fact that one Fl 265 was lost due to its refuelling being overlooked, the trials were a great success and augured well for the machine's place in naval reconnaissance and anti-submarine work. Other roles were also evaluated when an Fl 265 was used in exercises with Wehrmacht troops and performed such work as towing dinghies across a river and lifting bridge sections during construction. Although the Fl 265 had performed its duties well, had flown in adverse conditions and had no trouble going into and out of autorotation, natural doubts were expressed concerning its vulnerability to aerial attack. Consequently, a test was made in which a Messerschmitt Bf 109 and a Focke Wulf Fw 190 fitted with camera guns made determined simulated attacks on an Fl 265 for 20 minutes but failed to score one hit because of the helicopter's manoeuvrability. During the war, German fighters made similar but genuine attacks on a British rotorcraft but with the same lack of success.

The outcome of all these successes was that Flettner received instructions in 1940 to proceed with quantity production of the Fl 265, but, by that time, the design of a more advanced two-seat derivative of the Fl 265, the Fl 282, had been completed and the programme was switched to the new type. Thus, only the six prototypes of the Fl 265 were completed.

The pioneering work carried out in the field of rotary-wing aircraft by a German, Anton Flettner, is often overlooked and, perhaps for that reason, is particularly interesting. Seeking a way to overcome the torque induced when a rotor is driven from an airframe-mounted power source, Flettner explored the idea of putting a small engine and tractor propeller on each blade of a two-bladed rotor. This prototype helicopter made a successful tethered flight in 1932, but was destroyed shortly after on the ground when it overturned during a gale.

Flettner then built a two-seat Flettner Fl 184 autogyro with a three-bladed auto-rotating rotor and power provided by a 104kW Siemens-Halske Sh 14 radial engine driving a tractor propeller. This, too, was destroyed before it could be evaluated and the prototype Fl 185 followed, this being a combined autogyro/helicopter. Its Siemens-Halske engine, mounted at the fuselage nose, could be used to drive two variable-pitch propellers mounted on outriggers, one on each side of the fuselage, but the main rotor was powered only when required for operation in a helicopter mode. When flown as an autogyro the propellers on the out-riggers were both set to act as pushers and the main rotor auto-rotated. For helicopter flight the main rotor was powered from the engine and the outrigger propellers set so that one acted as a tractor and the other as a pusher to offset rotor torque.

The Fl 185 was only flown a few times before Flettner began construction, in 1937, of his Fl 265 VI prototype (D-EFLV), first flown in May 1939. This was of similar airframe configuration to the Fl 185, but dispensed with the outriggers and propellers, and introduced two two-bladed counter-rotating inter-meshing and synchronised main rotors which, because they were rotating in opposite directions, each cancelled the effects of the other's torque. To simplify control problems a tail unit incorporated an adjustable tailplane for trimming purposes, and for steering a large fin and rudder to augment the use of differential collective-pitch change on the two rotors. The aircraft was lost in an accident some three months later when the counter-rotating blades struck each other, but the Fl 265 V2 was used successfully for a variety of military trials. In all, six prototypes were built under contract to the German navy before, in 1940, an order was placed for quantity production. By then, however, Flettner had de signed a more advanced two-seat helicopter and it was decided instead to proceed with the development and manufacture of this improved aircraft.

Like the Fl 265, the Fl 282 underwent exhaustive service trials, and several were used operationally from 1942. Usually they flew from platforms above the gun turrets of convoy escort vessels in the Baltic, Aegean and Mediterranean, often in extreme weather conditions, and revealed control and performance qualities well above expectations. By VE-day, only three of the twenty-four prototypes completed by Flettner at Johannisthal still survived, the others having been destroyed to prevent capture. Two of these, the V15 and V23, were taken to the United States, and the other to the Soviet Union. The RLM had placed an order in 1944 for one thousand Fl 282's from BMW, but Allied bombing attacks prevented production from being started.

Upon the WWII conclusion, Anton Flettner was held in the "Dustbin" interrogation camp at Kransberg castle. After 1945, Flettner, along with many other aviation pioneers, was brought to the United States as part of Operation Paperclip. He started Flettner Aircraft Corporation, which developed helicopters for the US military. His company was not commercially successful, but his work was shared with the Army Air Corps. Many of his designs, such as intermeshing rotor concept, saw widespread use in a series of postwar helicopters built by Kaman for the US Navy and USAF. Anton Flettner moved to the United States in 1947 to work as a consultant to the Office of Naval research and became the chief designer of Kaman Aircraft, creating the Kaman HH-43 Huskie, a concept with intermeshing rotors. He died at age 76 in New York City, USA on December 29th, 1961 and buried in Eddersheim cemetery at Frankfurt, Germany where he was born.

At least two other Flettner helicopters were under development when the war ended. These were the Fl 285, another fleet spotter with an Argus As.10C engine, capable of making a 2-hour flight and carrying two small bombs; and the Fl 339, a large transport helicopter project powered by a BMW 132A engine.

Anton Flettner (2nd from left) meets Wernher von Braun (3rd from left).

Paul Baumgärtl

Paul Baumgarti was an Austrian who had worked on three helicopter designs during the war years before emigrating to Brazil. He experimented with a number of light helicopters in the 1950s and 1960s including the single-seat PB-60 unpowered ground-towed rotor kite, and the PB-64 which was an ultra-light single-seater with a minimal tubular fuselage structure. No production of any of these designs was undertaken.

Appendix B

Technical description of the Fl 282 B-0 and B-1 (as of 23. December 1943)

1. Purpose: I. Reconnaissance aircraft (land); II. Shipboard reconnaissance aircraft.

2. Designation: Fl 282 B-0 (with no cockpit glazing). Fl 282 B-1 (plexiglass glazed canopy).

3. Crew: one pilot

4. Design: Single-engined helicopter and gyroplane of mixed construction with two rotors.

(a) Fuselage: Welded steel tube, truss-type construction. Forward section with open (B-0) or enclosed (plexiglass] cockpit (B-1). Recess for back-type parachute in rear wall of seat. The fuselage center-section contains the entire power plant, the outer skin consists of removable doors, hoods and panels. Oval cross-section. The rear fuselage is fabric-covered with a rectangular cross-section.

(b) Rotor Blades: A tubular steel spar with riveted-on wooden ribs and plywood skin with fabric covering. Rectangular outline with rounded tips. Attached to rotor head with delta and alpha hinges. Receptacle for balance weight at end of spar (scrap). The axes of both rotors are angled outboard at 12° from the vertical. Seen from above, the right rotor rotates clockwise, the left counterclockwise.

(c) Control Surfaces: No elevator. Two-part horizontal stabilizer with single spar. Tubular steel spar with riveted-on wooden ribs. Plywood leading edge, fabric-covering, cantilever construction. Angle of incidence adjustable between -15 and +5° from cockpit.Rudder: wooden construction, fabric-covered, deflection to 40°. Vertical stabilizer: wooden construction with plywood leading edge and fabric covering, bolted to fuselage frame. No ailerons.

(d) Undercarriage: Braced fixed nosewheel with VDM oil shock-absorber leg, coupled with rudder foot pedals (steerable nosewheel). Nosewheel: EC tire 350 x 150mm. Mainwheels: EC tires 465 x 165mm.

5. Power Plant

(a) Engine Type: 1 BMW 314 E. Output: 160hp, compression ratio 1:6.0, rotor reduction ratio: 1:12.

(b) Transmission: Lower transmission flange-mounted on front of engine, in front cooling fan on extended crankshaft. Upper transmission, linked to the lower by a double cardan shaft. Firewall over and behind the engine.

(c) Fuel Tank: An unprotected metal tank located behind the firewall in the aft fuselage, consumable content 105 liters.

(d) Oil Tank: An unprotected 10-liter metal tank flange-mounted on the lower gearbox. Oil content of upper gearbox = 5l.

(e) Type of Fuel: 87 octane aviation gasoline.

(f) Cooling System: Continuous cooling provided by an eight-blade wooden cooling fan with direct drive from the engine. Oil cooler which is switched off for cold-weather operalion.

(g) Control System: Control about all three axes by means of periodic or constant changes in angle of incidence of the rotor blades by means of stick and rudder pedals, to which the rudder is connected. Change-over from helicopter to autogiro (autorotation) flight and reverse achieved by means of a speed-sensitive hydraulic regulator controlled by a hand-operated control lever; change-over to autorotation mode is automatic in the event of engine failure.

7. Equipment:

(a) Flight Instruments and Navigation Equipment: 1 airspeed indicator, 1 altimeter, 1 vertical speed indicator, 1 turn-and-bank indicator, 1 RPM indicator for rotors, 1 rotor blade angle indicator, 1 master compass, 1 dash-board clock.

(b) Safety and Rescue Equipment: 1 back-type parachute, 1 first-aid kit, 1 one-man inflatable raft (shipboard reconnaissance version).

(c) Radio and Signalling Equipment: 1 FuG 19 radio installation, 1 rigidly-mounted single-barrel flare pistol, 1 rigidly-mounted signal lamp (shipboard reconnaissance version).

(d) Bomb-Release Mechanism: 1 bomb magazine for two 5kg explosive devices (ship board reconnaissance version). 1 magazine for smoke buoys (shipboard reconnaissance version).

8. Special Equipment: Deck-landing equipment, consisting of: 1 tether with landing cable and electrical release.

9. Dimensions: Length of aircraft: 6150mm. Width, including undercarriage and tail surfaces: 2400mm. Height with rotor blades removed: 2400mm. Rotor diameter: 12000mm.

10. Technical Data:
(a) construction group: H 3;
(b) (b) maximum allowable flying weight: 1.000kg; (c) wing loading: 8.84 kg/m2 (based on rotor surface area);
(c) maximum allowable speeds: as helicopter: forward: 80 km/h, backward: 30km/h, sideways: 20km/h; as autogiro: 60km/h;
(e) minimum allowable speeds: as helicopter: no limitations; as autogiro: 40km/h, aerobatic forbidden!

11. Performance:
(a) Speed: Speed is temporarily limited to 80km/h in horizontal flight in helicopter mode for reasons of structural strength, 60km/h in autogiro mode.

(b) Rate of climb: 4.5m/s at sea level, 3.5m/s at 1000m, 3.0m/s at 1500m. Maximum altitude temporarily restricted to 1500 meters for flight safety reasons.

(c) Takeoff and Landing Performance: Takeoff and landing are made vertically. Autorotation landing in event of engine failure. Landing distance from height of 20m: 50m, stopping distance 15m (with wind speed of 5m/s).

12. Range: Endurance of 2 hours 5 minutes at maximum allowable speed of 80km/h and a range of 168km. The "Technical Description Fl 282 B-0 and B-1" presented above was prepared with the Fl 282V12.

Appendix C

Transportstaffel 40

The world's first helicopter squadron, was formed in the last months of the war to provide special transport and observation needs of the German Mountain Troops. Due to the chaotic times in the Spring of 1945, It was difficult for Transportstaffel 40 to effectively assemble its helicopters in one place let alone set up an effective operating group.

This article is designed to tell the story of this Staffel in the last months of the war and to the final disposition of its helicopters.

First some basic misconceptions about Transportstaffel 40:

It has been reported that this group actually performed rescues in encircled cities, observation, and artillery spotting before the war ended. This misconception has never been proven. In reality what few helicopters the group possessed spent almost all of their operational flying just trying to keep ahead of the rapidly advancing allies forces.

In the matter of unit insignias and unit codes, Transportstaffel 40 was never assigned a unit code. No reference to one is made in the formation order for the unit. No attempt was ever made to apply any unit markings

Unfortunately, no official documentation survives from Transportstaffel 40. All that survives of the units history is from the personal writing and interviews of its surviving members.

Transportstaffel 40 was ordered into existence in February of 1945. Hitler, convinced of the potential of the helicopter ordered the operational training be greatly accelerated. According to an OKL conference held in Berlin on February 12th, it was proposed to establish an operational helicopter test squadron. The Fa 223s coming from the Berlin-Tempelhof production line would be put at the Staffel's disposal. It was proposed that the unit would receive 35 helicopters by mid-1945 and increase by 30 per month. The unit was to become operational at Mühldorf as Transportstaffel 40 under the command of Hptm. Josef Stangl, who had attended the OKL conference on behalf of the General of the Transport Arm. The order to establish the unit, given on February 14, it was anticipated that the unit would reach full strength by March 10th.

The unit never reached full strength. Certainly it never received anything like the indicated number of Fa 223s.

After working up at Mühldorf, the unit quickly transferred to Ainring. In early March, six pilots and six radio operators attended the Alpine Warfare School in Fulpmes (near Innsbruck). At the same time, a number of mechanics also received technical training from Focke Achgelis.

Two Fl 282s were assigned to Transportstaffel 40 in early April. On April 10th, the first Fl 282 (V12) arrived piloted by Max Schmid. The next day Hans Fuisting (Flettner's head test pilot) ferried another Fl 282 (V11 or V22) to Ainring. Pilot Heinz Lex probably ferried a third Fl 282.

Little time was available for pilot training but the unit did manage to build a tethering device using cement blocks so that a primitive form of ground training was possible.

On April 10th, an order had been issued for Focke Archelis pilot Hans Gerstenhauer to ferry the Fa 223 V14 to the unit. The V14 would soon be joined by a second Fa 223, the V51 which had been at Rechlin since mid-March and which was transferred to Transportstaffel 40 by Otto Dumke.

In the early hours of April 20th, a small detachment of pilots and mechanics from Transportstaffel 40 set out northwards to collect two additional Fa 223s (V52 and V53) from the Focke Achgelis production line at Berlin-Tempelhof. Continuous air raids an over Berlin and heavy Soviet shelling prevented the intended completion of these helicopters, which together with the largely complete V54 and 15 or so others in varying stages, would be captured by the Red Army on April 26th.

On April 22nd, the detachment decided to return to Ainring from Berlin. It was during the return flight that one of Transportstaffel pilots, Heinz Lux, was shot down in his Fi 156 by ground troops and he was sequentially captured the the Americans.

On April 26th, Hans Fuisting arrived in Ainring in the Fl 282 V23. He soon left with Flettner pilot Ernst Remain in the Fl 282 V12 for Flettner's new facility in Bad Tölz. Once these two Fl 282s reached Bad Tölz, they were dismantled and hidden away pending the arrival of the Allied Forces.

Given the chaotic conditions, there was no opportunity for any new pilots to be trained on the Fa 223. On April 23rd, Gerstenhauer received orders from Fl. Gen. Ing. Rudolf Herrmann, that he would be required to perform support missions for the German Mountain Troops at Hochkönig. However the absence of any freight-loading equipment such a mission would be impractical. Gerstenhauer sought to rectify the situation by acquring the needed equipment from Focke Achgelis facility in Ochsenhausen. However, unknown to Gerstenhauer, the Focke Achgelis facility was in the process of being evacuated to Obermaiselstein.

On April 24th, Gerstenhauer set out by car for Ochsenhausen. Upon reaching Oberammergau, he was advised that the French had reached Wuttemberg and that an Fa 223 was seen flying in the direction of Mittenwald. Gerstenhauer deducted that this could only have been Carol Bode in the Fa 223 V16, who was scheduled to deliver the V16 to Transportstaffel 40.

Gerstenhauer, with no hope of reaching Focke Achgelis, turned his attention to finding Bode. He caught up with him near the village of Scharnitz on April 25th. There the two meet and discussed the impending future. Bode recalls instructing Gerstenhauer to make sure the V14 did not fall into Allied hands and passed on the order to blow up the helicopter at all cost. Gerstenhauer disputes this order, recalling that he instructed Bode that he would return to Ainring and try to organize their fuel supplies in order to provide support for the German Mountain troops in the area. Neither men would see each other again before the end of hostilities.

Bode then fly the Fa 223 V16 to the Eppzirl Valley shortly before the arrival of American troops. It was there with the help of his mechanic Rudolf, that they destroyed the Fa 223 V16 and buried what they could of the remains. These remains could still be seen in the valley into the 1960s.

On April 27th, instructions were given by the OKL that all available helicopters, along with all remaining Fiesler Fi 156s and a number of Junckers Ju 88 night fighters and Heinkel He 111s, were required to assemble into liaison Staffen on airfields in the Innsbruck, Aigen-Zeltweg and southern Alpine areas in the defense of the Alpine Stronghold. Since no infrastructure existed, there was no chance for a last stand to be put in place. In reality, there was nothing to do but await the end.

On April 30th, the ground unit of Transportstaffel 40 set out for Aigen. It was agreed that the helicopters would also leave that day. With the loss of Lux, Transportstaffel 40 was left with one qualified Fl 282 pilot (Schimd). It was decided that Schmid would fly the V22 to Aigen on the 30th then return to Ainring by car in order to fly the V11 to Aigen.

One May 2nd, the Fa 223 V11 piloted by Gerstenhauer, the Fl 282 V11 flown by Schmid and the Fl 223 V51 , flown by Dumke(?), left for Aigen.

At Aigen, conditions were less then satisfactory. The Staff of Luftwaffe Command 17 and Luftwaffe Command 4 had also relocated to Aigen. This airfield was built to support 600 people, but now housed some 2,500. Despite wide spread looting, Transportstaffel 40 commander Stangl was able to secure supplies for his men For security, the helicopters made a short transfer flight to Seebacherhf on the north bank of the Putterersee bordering the airport.

There Schmid made a number of reconnaissance flights, endeavoring to establish further landing sites and determining the extent of the Soviet armies advance.

By May 7th, the Soviets were less then 19 miles away and orders were received to transfer westward to avoid capture. On the 8th the ground element of Transportstaffel 40 set out by road to Zell-am-See. Since there was no pilot for the Fl 282 V11, attempts were made to destroy the craft and it was pushed into the Putterersee. The remaining Fl 282 and the two Fa 223s set out for Lend, their agreed upon rendezvous point. It was there that the pilots learned of the Armistice.

Schmid in the Fa 223 V51 then flew to locate the ground support convoy of Transportstaffel 40, and he eventually caught up with them near Radstadt, but was unable to make contact as the ground support convoy was entirely enter meshed with the fleeing German Army. Schmidt had no choice but to return to Schwarzach/St. Veit.

The ground support convoy with Stangl eventually reached Salzburg where they surrendered to American troops.

At Schwarzach/St. Veit, the pilots and crew of the three remaining helicopters weighed their options. Capture and interrogation seemed inevitable. They felt they had only two choices, destroy their machines and try to get to there families by foot, or surrender to the Americans, where they felt there expertise with the helicopters would put them in a better negotiating position. Dumke and Gerstenhauer decided on the later and with their remaining fuel fly their Fa 223s back to Ainring to surrender to the Americans.

Schmid decided not to join the other pilots, instead opting to fly the Fl 282 V22 to his home village of Wallern (about 80 miles south east of Vienna) to rejoin his wife. On May 9th, Schmid landed at his family farm house and with the help of his wife hide the Fl 282 in the barn. His flight did not go unnoticed. Soon American troops arrived and took Schmid prisoner. Schmid refused to fly the Fl 282 for the Americans. Instead he helped them dismantle the Fl 282 for a longer voyage. unfortunately nothing is know as to the fate of the Fl 282 V22.

Rising early on May 9th Gerstenhauer and Dumke and their passengers left for Aining. Ainring had been occupied by American troops of the 414th Armored Field Artillery Battalion of the 20th Armored Division of the US A 7th Army. The arrival of the two German helicopters on the 9th, startled the American troops, who unceremoniously hauled the pilots and their passengers out of their helicopters.

As a footnote both Gerstenhauer and Dumke were to interest the Allies in their expertise and continued to work and fly their helicopters for the allies after the war.

Appendix D

Type IX A

Of the Type IX U-boats the D1 and the D2 had the Flettner Fl 330 Wagtail onboard. An overview of the different Type IX.

U 37 to U 44 = 8 U-boats

This U-boat type was developed as a dubble-hull unit on the basis of U 81 of the Imperial German Navy (1915) and Kriegsmarine Type I A.

Year of construction 1936 to 1939
Shipyard AG Weser at Bremen
Displacement 1,032 t/ 1,152 t submerged
Length 76.5 m
Beam 6.5 m
Draught 4.7 m
Propulsion 2 Diesel engines, 2 electric engines, 2 propellers
Engine power 4,400 HP/ 1,000 HP submerged
Speed 18.2 kn/ 7.7 kn submerged
Range 8,100 nmi at 12 kn/ 65 nmi at 4 kn submerged
Diving depth 230 m
Fuel 154 cbm
Armament 4 bow and 2 stern torpedo tubes, 22 torpedoes or 14 torpedoes and up to 42 mines, 1 x 10.5 cm, 1 x 3.7 cm guns, later 4 x 2 cm twin mounts
Complement 48 – later more

Type IX B

U 64, U 65, U 103 to U 111, U 122 to U 124 = 14 U-boats

The U-boat was a further development of Type IX A to accommodate several improvements.

Year of construction 1937 to 1940
Shipyard AG Weser at Bremen
Displacement 1.051 t/ 1.178 t submerged
Length 76.5 m

Beam 6.8 m
Draught 4.7 m

Propulsion 2 Diesel engines, 2 electric engines, 2 propellers
Engine power 4,400 HP/ 1,000 HP submerged
Speed 18.2 kn/ 7.7 kn submerged
Range 8,700 nmi at 12 kn/ 64 nmi at 4 kn submerged
Diving depth 230 m
Fuel 165 cbm
Armament 4 bow and 2 stern torpedo tubes, 22 torpedoes or 14 torpedoes and to zu 42 mines, 1 x 10.5 cm, 1 x 3.7 cm guns, later twin 4 x 2 cm
Complement 48 – later more

Type IX C and IX C/40

U 66 to U 68/ U 125 to U 131/ U 153 to U 176/ U 183 to U 194/ U 501 to U 550/ U 801 to U 806/ U 841 to U 846/ U 853 to U 858/ U 865 to U 870/ U 877 to U 881/ U 889/ U 1221 to U 1235= 140 U-boats

This U-boat type was a further development of Type IX A, respectively IX B with enlarged conning tower. It was later fittet with a snorkel.

Year of construction 1940 to 1944
Shipyard U 66 to U 68/ U 125 to U 131/ U 153 to U 160/ U 171 to U 176/ U 183 to U 194/ U 841 to U 846/ U 853 to U 858/ U 865 to U 870/ U 877 to U 881/ U 889 at AG Weser at Bremen,

U 161 to U 170/ U 801 to U 806 at Seebeck at Wesermünde,
U 501 to U 550/ U 1221 to U 1235 at Deutsche Werft at Hamburg

Displacement IX C = 1.120 t/ 1.232 t submerged, IX C/40 = 1.144 t/ 1.257 t submerged
Length 76.5 m
Beam 6.8 m
Draught 4.7 m
Propulsion 2 Diesel engines, 2 electric engines, 2 propellers
Engine power 4,400 HP/ 1,000 HP submerged
Speed IX C = 18,2 kn/ 7,7 kn submerged, IX C/40 = 18,3 kn/ 7,3 kn submerged
Range 11.000 nmi at 12 kn/ 63 nmi at 4 kn submerged
Diving depth 230 m
Fuel 208 cbm

Armament 4 bow and 2 stern torpedo tubes, 22 torpedoes or to zu 42 mines, 1 x 10.5 cm, 1 x 3.7 cm guns, later twin 4×2 cm , U 162 to U 170 and U 505 to U 550 had no minelaying capacity
Complement 48 – later more

Type IX D 1

U 180 and U 195 = 2 U-boats

This U-boat Type was built as a particular powerful combat unit by extending the pressure hull´s length while maintaining it´s diameter. Initially these two units were equipped with two sets of three side-by-side Daimler Benz 20 cylinder diesel Engines (same as in German Fast Attack Crafts) and a Vulcan gearbox generating 9,000 HP for 20.8 kn surfaced. 1943 the U-boats were refitted with standard diesel engines to serve as a fuel supply unit.

Year of construction 1940 to 1942
Shipyard AG Weser at Bremen
Displacement 1,610 t/ 1,804 t submerged
Length 87.6 m
Beam 7.5 m
Draught 5.4 m
Propulsion 2 Diesel engines, 2 electric engines, 2 propellers
Engine power 4,400 HP/ 1,000 HP submerged, after refitting: 2,800 HP/ 1,110 HP submerged
Speed 20.8 kn/ 6.9 kn submerged, after refitting = 15.8 kn/ 6.9 kn submerged
Range 23,700 nmi at 12 kn/ 57 nmi at 4 kn submerged/ after refitting: 9,900 nmi at 12 kn/ 115 nmi at 4 kn submerged
Diving depth 230 m
Fuel 203 cbm plus 253 cbm Treibstoff für Fremdversorgung
Armament 4 bow and 2 stern torpedo tubes, 24 torpedoes or up to 39 mines, 1 x 10.5 cm, 1 x 3.7 cm guns, later twin 4 x 2 cm, after refitting no torpedo tubes and no minelaying capacity any longer
Complement 57 – later more

Type IX D 2

U 177 to U 179/ U 181 and U 182/ U 196 to U 200/ U 847 to U 852/ U 859 to U 864/ U 871 to U 876/ U 883 = 29 U-boats

These were combat units for long range operations in the Indian Ocean and Far East. It was fitted wth two Diesel generators with 1.00 HP additionally which could be operated together with the two main engines during diesel-electric mode of operation providing for a very long ranhe that could reach up to 31,500 nmi at 10 kn. Therefore these U-boats were able to circumnavigate the Earth without refuelling.

Year of construction 1940 to 1944
Shipyard AG Weser at Bremen
Displacement 1,610 t/ 1,804 t submerged
Length 87.6 m
Beam 7.5 m
Draught 5.4 m
Propulsion 2 Diesel engines plus 2 Dieselgeneratoren, 2 electric engines, 2 propellers
Engine power 4,400 HP/ 1,000 HP submerged
Speed 19.2 kn/ 6.9 kn submerged
Range 23,700 nmi at 12 kn/ 57 nmi at 4 kn submerged
Diving depth 230 m
Fuel 441 cbm
Armament 4 bow and 2 stern torpedo tubes, 24 torpedoes or up to 39 mines, 1 x 10.5 cm, 1 x 3.7 cm guns, later only 1x 3.7 cm plus 2 x 2 cm twins
Complement 57 – later more

Literature

Coates, Steve and Carbonel, Jean-Christophe. Helicopters of the Third Reich. Crowborough, UK: Classic Publications Ltd., 2002. ISBN 1-903223-24-5.

Fa 223...Henrich Focke's Singular Kite, Part One. Air International, May 1984, Vol. 26 No. 5. Bromley, UK:Pilot Press. pp. 245–247, 259–262. ISSN 0306-5634.

Fa 223...Henrich Focke's Singular Kite, Part Two. Air International, June 1984, Vol. 26 No. 6. Bromley, UK:Pilot Press. pp. 291–296. ISSN 0306-5634.

Ford, Roger (2013). Germany's Secret Weapons of World War II. London, United Kingdom: Amber Books. p. 224. ISBN 9781909160569

Green, William. The Warplanes of the Third Reich. Galahad Books, 1990. ISBN 0-88365-666-3.

Kay, Antony L.; J. Richard Smith (2002). German Aircraft of the Second World War: Including Helicopters and Missiles. Annapolis, MD: Naval Institute Press. ISBN 978-1557500106.

Nowarra, Heinz J. German Helicopters, 1928-1945. Atglen, Pennsylvania: Schiffer Publishing, 1990. ISBN 0-88740-289-5.

Nowarra, Heinz J.. Die Deutsche Luftruestung 1933-1945 - Vol.1 - AEG-Dornier. Bernard & Graefe Verlag. 1993. Koblenz. ISBN 3-7637-5464-4 (Gesamtwek), ISBN 3-7637-5465-2 (Band 1)

Polmar, Norman and Floyd D. Kennedy. Military Helicopters of the World: Military Rotary-wing Aircraft Since 1917. Naval Institute Press, 1981. ISBN 0-87021-383-0.

Sampson, Anthony The Sovereign State of ITT, Stein and Day, 1973, ISBN 0-8128-1537-8

Smith, J. Richard. Focke-Wulf, an Aircraft Album. London: Ian Allan, 1973. ISBN 0-7110-0425-0.

Smith, J. Richard and Kay, Anthony. German Aircraft of the Second World War. London: Putnam & Company 1972 (3rd edition 1978). ISBN 0-370-00024-2.

The Illustrated Encyclopedia of Aircraft (Part Work 1982-1985). Orbis Publishing.

Witkowski, Ryszard. Rotorcraft of the Third Reich. Redbourn, UK: Mushroom Model Publications, 2007. ISBN 978-83-89450-43-2.

Made in the USA
Monee, IL
06 November 2023

45853826R00077